Making Ends Meet & Dreams Come True

Success Guide for Better Money Management

6th Edition

BY

GARY TAGTMEIER, CPA
BOB GORSKY, PhD

FINANCIAL AWARENESS® INSTITUTE

Making Ends Meet ... and Dreams Come True
By Bob Gorsky, PhD and Gary Tagtmeier, CPA
© 1993-2003 Financial Awareness® Institute, 6th Edition (November 2003).
ISBN 0-9746303-0-6

This book is one of the *Making Ends Meet and Dreams Come True* series of guidebooks for better money management. This book was developed in cooperation with the Whitman Corporation, Financial Awareness® Institute and HPN WorldWide®.

Financial Awareness® Institute
900 Jorie Boulevard • Suite 110
Oak Brook, IL 60521
630/963-7000 • 630/990-1775 (FAX)
www.financialinfoportal.com

Making Ends Meet ... and Dreams Come True

About the Authors

Gary Tagtmeier, CPA, is a Certified Public Accountant with over 32 years of experience consulting individuals about personal money management. As President of the Financial Awareness® Institute, over the last 23 years he has worked with major corporations conducting financial education programs across the country for their employees and family members. In addition, he has worked with the U.S. Military, benefits consulting firms, employee assistance programs and financial institutions across the country. Gary and his wife (Mary Ann) have three children (Gwen, Betsy and Elliot).

Bob Gorsky, PhD, has a doctorate in health promotion and human performance with over 27 years of experience helping people in the areas of prevention, early detection, decision support and personal improvement to achieve greater success in health, family work, financial and other areas of life. He is the Founder and President of HPN WorldWide®, Inc. (www.hpn.com) working with employers, insurance companies and community groups throughout the world. He is also a member of the Consumer Information and Education Committee of the Midwest Business Group on Health, and works with employee assistance programs and specialists, business groups, professional associations, schools and community outreach groups. He speaks regularly at national conferences. Bob and his wife (Barb) have three children (Sara, Ben and Sean).

The combined insights, expertise and experience of the authors are what make this book unique. Money management is approached from the perspectives of financial, psychological, lifestyle and family management like never before!

Acknowledgments

A special thanks to all of the following people who have assisted in the development (via suggestions, reviews and/or editing) of this guidebook: Pat Stahl, Diane Zack, Tammy Alberico, Ray Werntz, Joe DeRosa, Don Kemper, Tony Herron, Marjorie Boehmler, Barb Gorsky, Mary Ann Tagtmeier, Socrates Annes, Linda Bieniek, Ginnie Brickley, Clare Corbett, Jim Denny, Bern Drzastwa, Loretta Drzastwa, Steve Easterday, Conney Ewing, Bob Force, Denny Franseen, Tim Freund, Ruth Govoni, Emmett Herr, Charlie Jordan, Marshall Jowars, Don Keiser, Mike Lada, Don McClenehan, Gerre Nadig, Betty Pflaumer, John Ringer, Ellen Rosen, Johnnie Ross-Williams, Gil Sanks, Carole Segatti, Tom Spicer, Cynthia Sweeney, Roger Tagtmeier, Doug Thompson, Ernie Thompson, Neil Thompson, Nancy Urquhart, Pat Zar, Dan Zimmerman, Vince Holt and many more. We thank the directors, advisors and progressive corporations which have worked with us and allowed us to assist their employees.

Design & Artwork Credits • Desk-Top-Publishing by Health Promotion Network, Inc. and HPN WorldWide in Elmhurst, Illinois • ClickArt® Images Copyright ©1990 T/Maker Company from ClickArt® Business Cartoons by T/Maker Company in Mountain View, California. • Desk Top Art™ by Dynamic Graphics in Peoria, Illinois. • Cover by Dave Johnson at Graphic Communication Technologies in Oak Brook, IL.

About the Financial Awareness Institute and this Book

The Financial Awareness® Institute is dedicated to helping people manage their personal finances. Inflation, constant tax law changes, and employer benefit changes are just some reasons why people need help. Also, we have found that most people never received money management education in their schooling. Since 1980, Financial Awareness ® Institute has worked with major corporations and unions across the country to educate their employees and members about personal money management. From this experience, we have developed the following five "Basic Beliefs" about people and their money:

1) Most people could manage their financial resources better;
2) Objective, ongoing education is essential to improved personal money management;
3) People have different needs at different stages of their financial lifecycle;
4) The rules will always change! and
5) Effective personal money management requires a realistic starting point, a long-term vision and a plan.

These beliefs are the foundation of our mission which is to provide education and solutions to personal financial events that affect people. This book will help you determine your underlying attitude towards money and the things that are important to you. Understanding your personal beliefs, using your personal resources to their utmost and gaining control over your money instead of letting money control you, is critical. This will allow you to enjoy life at any financial level.

Note to the Reader

The Financial Awareness® Institute is an educational organization with the sole purpose of simplifying financial information for individuals. Financial Awareness® was founded with the concept of providing objective personal financial information without conflicts of interest. It does not endorse any lending, insurance, accounting or legal organizations; therefore, its information is uniquely unbiased. However, the information contained within this guidebook is subject to change because of ongoing changes in our laws, economy and financial community at local, state, federal and even worldwide levels. We strive to keep up with these changes and to update future editions of guidebooks accordingly. The information within this guidebook should not be considered professional legal, investment, tax or accounting advice. What we share with you is general information on money management. There may be times in your life when it would be wise to seek competent professional help from qualified professionals in these areas to assist in financial planning.

Chapter 1

Where did you learn to manage money?

Life is like a business.

You are the "Big Cheese."

Traits of good presidents.

Where do you stand?

Views vary.

Exercise 1.1: The Bottom-Line

Chapters to read--based on your situation.

$ $ $ $ $ $ $ $ $ $ $

The Bottom Line

Where did you learn to manage money?

Throughout life "here and there" is where most of us picked up our ideas about managing money and financial success. Family, friends, TV shows, business teachers and insurance agents may have been just a few of our sources.

Most of us have little formal training in the area of money management. We have been on our own to learn the facts of life and money —often the hard way.

This workbook attempts to fill the gap and keep you from scraping your knees while traveling the road of money and life. It offers you tools and ideas to help you become a better president of YOU, Inc. and partner of FAMILY, Inc.

Life can be compared to many things. It can be like a roller coaster, mountain climbing, a breeze, the pits, like ballooning and a journey with many pathways.

Life is like a business.

Your life is also like a business. You bring money in —a lot of money over a lifetime. Career-wise, a person making an average $25,000 a year brings in $1,000,000 over 40 years. Just as businesses do, you use money for many purposes —most often for necessities, but also for making improvements. At one time or another, most of us have probably thrown some away.

If you don't take care of your operations, you'll probably spend more time and money trying to fix the things that are breaking down. This goes for your car, home, health, and family.

You
are the
BIG
CHEESE.

You are the president of YOU, Inc.

You oversee almost all of your operations: You decide what to put in your mouth, when to sleep, how to work with others, when to get help, how to use your time —the list is endless. You might have an advisory board, hopefully, to make wiser decisions.

If you're single and on your own, you also decide how to make money and what to do with your money.

If you're married, things get a little more complicated. You are also a chief partner in FAMILY, Inc. Making decisions about money and other family operations then becomes a team effort. These are in addition to your responsibilities as president of YOU, Inc.

Traits of Good Presidents

Most good presidents and partners know what to look for at the bottom line. But they also know to look deeper. They work to keep aware of all the operations in the business that affect the bottom line. They know how to work with people.

Good presidents and partners have and use a good advisory board. Financially, they value wise counsel on legal, tax, insurance and investment matters —especially at critical times in the business. We can benefit from this same advice at certain times, such as: when getting married, having kids, with changes in income, job loss, at retirement, with divorce, death of family members or friends and other major life events.

Good presidents and partners have thoughtful vision, goals, action plans, courage and discipline. Most importantly they have high standards in everything they do. They strive to make the business stronger. They strive to avoid foolish decisions that could harm or ruin their business.

Where do you stand?

Where do you stand as the president of YOU, Inc. and as a partner of FAMILY, Inc?

How are you doing financially? Are you doing well, breaking even or going down the tubes? Do you really know how you're doing or are you guessing? How do you feel about where you are? Proud, shrewd, concerned, worried, depressed or indifferent? It's a matter of opinion and a matter of perspective.

Views vary.

People have different ideas of what it means to be in good financial shape.

Some people grew up in the depression era. Many of these people may feel like they are in financial trouble if they cannot pay cash for everything they buy. They may always be worried about money. Others feel like they are in trouble if they are late in paying a few bills.

On the other side, there are those who are late in paying their bills, have credit card balances to the maximum, pay the minimum amounts due and do not feel like they are in trouble. In fact, they may feel they are in great financial shape!

As most of us know, feelings do not always correspond with the facts. Many of us don't know what facts to look for, what they mean or how to feel about them. The upcoming exercise should help.

Exercise 1.1: The Bottom-Line

The exercise in this section offers you the chance to assess some of the bottom line indicators of your financial side of life. How you score on this will give you an idea of where you currently are, and where you could be in the future. This exercise is also like a map. It will help you to navigate through this book knowing what chapters need more of your attention than others.

Answer each question. Then add up the points for each answer you circled. At the end of this chapter there are further instructions for making more sense out of your answers and total score, and how to use them to navigate through this workbook.

Exercise 1.1 • The Bottom Line ... *Money-Wise, This Is Your Life !*

<u>Points</u>

1. My rent or mortgage is:

   A. I have no rent or mortgage payments. — 10
   B. Always paid on time. — 9
   C. Almost always paid on time. However, occasionally payments have been late and I have paid penalties. — 8
   D. Often paid on time. However, many payments have been late and I have paid penalties. — 5
   E. Usually paid late, including penalties. — 3
   F. More than one month behind and I have been warned of the possibility of eviction or foreclosure. — 1

2. My car payment(s) are:

   A. I have no car payments. — 10
   B. Always paid on time. — 9
   C. Usually made on time. However, I have paid some late with penalties. — 8
   D. Often paid on time. However, a good number of payments have been late and I have paid penalties. — 5
   E. Regularly late, and I frequently pay late penalties. — 3
   F. More than one month behind and the lender is threatening to repossess my car. — 1

3. My credit card bills are:

   A. Always paid in full. — 10
   B. Almost always paid in full. When I can't, I always pay <u>much more</u> than the minimum due. — 8
   C. Almost always paid in full. When I can't, I usually pay the <u>minimum due</u> --or maybe <u>a little more</u>. — 6
   D. I regularly pay only the minimum monthly amount due on one or more of my credit cards. — 2
   E. I am receiving letters and phone calls from credit card companies for late, under, or no payments. — 1

4. My utilities (phone, water, gas and electric) are:

   A. Always paid on time. — 10
   B. Usually paid on time. However, I have paid some late penalties. — 8
   C. Regularly late and I pay whatever late penalties there are. — 5
   D. The utility companies are threatening to shut off my phone, water, gas and/or electric. — 1

5. Taxes:

   A. I send in my income tax form and pay whatever is due on time every year. — 10
   B. I am usually late filing my income tax and have to pay penalties on taxes due for filing late. — 6
   C. I am losing sleep over some risky things I have done to reduce my taxes that might result in an audit, or the IRS coming after me within the next three years. — 4
   D. The IRS is threatening to attach liens to my bank account. — 1

6. Debts:

A. I have no debts or loans (from banks, credit unions, family, friends, casinos, etc.).	10
B. I have one or more loans, my payments are prompt, and I am paying the loans off ahead of schedule.	8
C. I have one or more loans, my payments are usually prompt, and I am not paying the loans off early.	6
D. I am considering a loan consolidation package.	4
E. I borrow money from friends and relatives for food and other necessities.	1

7. Environmental actions (regarding utilities, travel, purchases, waste, work, fuel, play, etc.):

A. I consider myself very environmental and energy conscious regarding the way I live and manage my money. I fix and maintain things, recycle, use less energy and do many other things to save resources and money.	10
B. I am just beginning to become a little more environmentally conscious. I am beginning to fix and maintain things, recycle, use less energy and do a few other things to save resources and money but I have a long way to go.	6
C. I think this environmental stuff has been blown way out of proportion. I should be able to live life the way I want, with all the comforts of prior generations--and more! If people can afford to, they should replace it or toss it.	1

8. If I* were to lose my job today, I have enough in easily reachable (liquid) savings (not including retirement savings and investments) that would last for this many months of regular living expenses:

A. 12 or more months	10
B. 6-11 months	8
C. 1-5 months	4
D. less than 1 month	1

* *If married, assume spouse is not working either.*

9. Personal relationships:

A. I'm not married and don't live with anyone.	10
B. We have never (or rarely) had problems discussing money matters. We both know our financial situation and goals and work together to manage our money well.	10
C. We don't have any major money problems, but we could do better discussing and working together to manage our money better.	8
D. We have occasional problems regarding money or even just knowing what our financial situation is. This is putting a drain on our relationship.	6
E. We have frequent problems regarding money. These are severely threatening our relationship.	1

10. I spend about this much on alcohol at grocery stores, liquor stores, bars, lounges and elsewhere:	A. Not even a penny.	10
	B. Less than $5 per week or less than $20 per month	10
	C. $5-$10 per week or $20-$40 per month	8
	D. $10-$20 per week or $40-$80 per month	4
	E. More than $20 per week or more than $80 per month.	1

11. On the average, I spend this much playing lottos, cards, slot machines, bingo, races, sports events, and other forms of gambling:	A. Not even a penny.	10
	B. Less than $26 the whole year (usually: when the lotto's big, or on my rare trip to the races, etc.).	8
	C. $1-$5 per week or $4-$20 per month.	6
	D. $6-$10 per week or $24-$40 per month.	4
	E. more than $10 per week or more than $40 per month.	1

12. I spend about this much on illegal drugs:	A. Not even a penny.	10
	B. $1-$5 per day or $7-$35 per week	3
	C. $6-$10 per day or $42-$70 per week	2
	D. $11-$20 per day or $77-$140 per week	1
	E. more than $20 per day or more than $140 per week	0

13. Attitude toward drugs:	A. I refuse to use any illegal drugs--no matter what the peer pressure, situation or burdens of life may be.	10
	B. If my "friends encourage" me, I am open to personally experimenting with various illegal drugs in the future	4
	C. I occasionally use one or more illegal drugs	1
	D. I regularly use one or more illegal drugs	0

14. As far as legal documents go:	A. I have a will and a living will.	10
	B. I have either a will or a living will, but not both.	8
	C. I don't have either, but have been thinking about one or the other and will have them soon.	5
	D. I don't have either kind of will and am not too worried about it.	1

15. For the most part, I buy things this way:	A. Usually in cash or by check (or occasionally on credit), when I believe it's a wise choice, after I've considered my checkbook, savings, ability to pay for it, budget, personal financial goals and needs. When I am spontaneous, it's sensible.	10
	B. If I think I can afford it, I buy it, usually based on my feelings, emotions and mood of the moment. I enjoy being spontaneous when I buy things, and a budget makes me feel uncomfortable.	6
	C. When I want or need something, I buy it and usually worry about paying the credit card bills later. I don't have a budget or consider the future.	1

16. Out of my monthly income I regularly save or invest about:

A. over $500 per month	10
B. $200-$500 per month	8
C. $100-$199 per month	6
D. $1-$99 per month	4
E. I am not saving anything, but I am breaking even.	2
F. I am not saving anything, and must borrow money, food, shelter or other things to make it.	1

17. If I were to get a fairly large sum of money or stock (as a gift, inheritance, or when leaving a company due to restructuring, retirement or other reasons), I would:

A. Think carefully about my retirement and other future goals, tax and other considerations before deciding what to do with the money.	10
B. Think carefully about my retirement and other future goals, tax and other considerations before deciding how to cash it in and spend it.	6
C. Get the things I always wanted or needed, because my social security and pension should be enough to take care of me in retirement.	1

18. This is the way I view my 401K, IRAs and other tax-deferred savings and investments I might have:

A. It's for retirement and I do not intend to touch it, other than to make changes in investments or funds to get the best returns from the stock market.	10
B. It's for retirement and I do not intend to touch it. I see others making changes with their funds, but I don't really know what to do, so I just leave my funds alone.	8
C. It is not just for retirement. It's also for major future goals regarding education (for me or kids), home improvements, new purchases, emergencies, etc.	6
D. It's like a savings account, to be used for regular living expenses or to pay taxes. I count on it often to make ends meet, even though it's difficult to get the money out.	2

19. If I were to die right now, my survivors (including any of my children under the age of 21) should have enough money (through savings, investments, insurance and wills) to :

A. I have no immediate survivors to provide for, but there would be at least enough to pay off all my debts.	10
B. Pay off the house, meet regular living expenses for 15 or more years, <u>and</u> cover most expenses of each family member getting a college or trade school degree.	10
C. Pay off the house, meet regular living expenses for the next 5-14 years, <u>and</u> cover most expenses of each family member getting a college or trade school degree.	8
D. Meet regular living expenses for 6 or more years (including the house payment), <u>and</u> cover most expenses of each family member getting a college or trade school degree.	6
E. Meet regular living expenses for the next 1-5 years, and cover most expenses of each family member getting a college or trade school degree.	4
F. Meet regular living expenses for the next 1-5 years, but I doubt if anyone could afford to go to any college or trade school.	3
G. I don't know how long the money would last, but it would probably be less than a year--and all the debts could not be paid off.	1
H. I don't know.	0

20. If someone were to ask me right now about my money (how I manage it, about my budget and expenses, investments and returns, philosophies toward money, etc.)-- if I could trust them and felt like telling them I could:

A. Provide them with accurate details about each of these--between what I know off the top of my head, and the records, receipts and plans that I keep.   **10**

B. Tell them a few things about some of these--between what I've been thinking about, my records, receipts and files. But I have not really thought deeply about or put on paper some of these things.   **6**

C. Guess at a few of these and say "I don't know" or exaggerate a lot. Quite honestly, I haven't really thought a lot about these things and haven't put it on paper--and any receipts or records I may still have aren't really organized.   **1**

Add the points for your answers and enter total here

INTERPRET YOUR SCORE

Here are a few ways to interpret and use your scores.

As you may have already deduced, the higher your score the better money manager you probably are and the better financial shape you are in. This goes for the score for each question as well as your total score.

The lower your score, the more you are risking financial problems, stress and even disaster. The lower your score, the more opportunities there are for improvement, and the more effort it will take to turn your situation around. But don't despair, it can be done.

Even if your score is high, you can still improve. The need may not be as urgent, but the opportunities are still there. People with higher scores are probably doing most of the things that people with lower scores need to do.

On the next page, plot your score on your mountain of wealth and life to see how far you have already climbed on the path of money management.

You may be near the top, which means you've done a lot of work already. You've worked hard and can feel a sense of accomplishment as you look back on life.

If you are closer to the bottom, you have more climbing to do. But, not any more than the person above you has had to climb. It just means you have to catch up with the people who have already climbed higher.

Resist being discouraged by a low score. Choose to focus on making the successes and progress of others more inspiring to you. This focus can energize you and your efforts to move forward and improve. If they can do it, you can too!

Plot your total score below and see where you stand.

Then, check the next page for a few tips on where to focus your efforts.

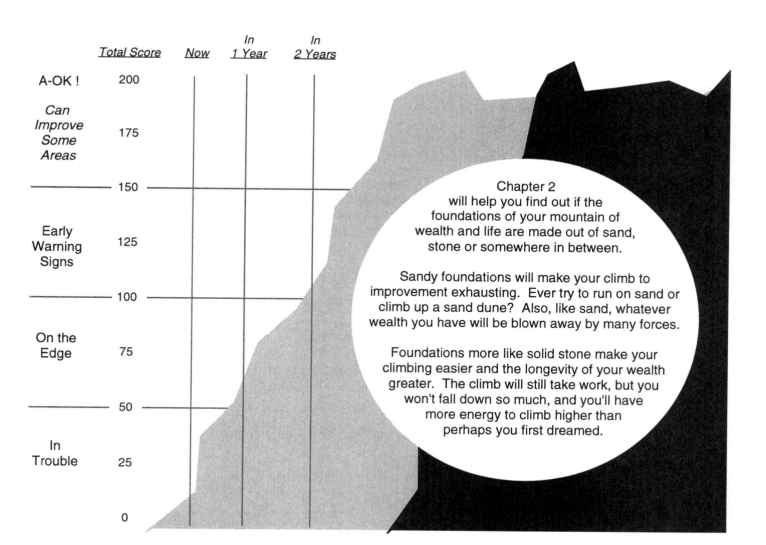

	Total Score	Now	In 1 Year	In 2 Years
A-OK !	200			
Can Improve Some Areas	175			
	150			
Early Warning Signs	125			
	100			
On the Edge	75			
	50			
In Trouble	25			
	0			

Chapter 2 will help you find out if the foundations of your mountain of wealth and life are made out of sand, stone or somewhere in between.

Sandy foundations will make your climb to improvement exhausting. Ever try to run on sand or climb up a sand dune? Also, like sand, whatever wealth you have will be blown away by many forces.

Foundations more like solid stone make your climbing easier and the longevity of your wealth greater. The climb will still take work, but you won't fall down so much, and you'll have more energy to climb higher than perhaps you first dreamed.

Depending upon your situation, you may need to pay more attention to certain chapters before others.

Simply check below for some ideas on where you need to focus your attention and efforts.

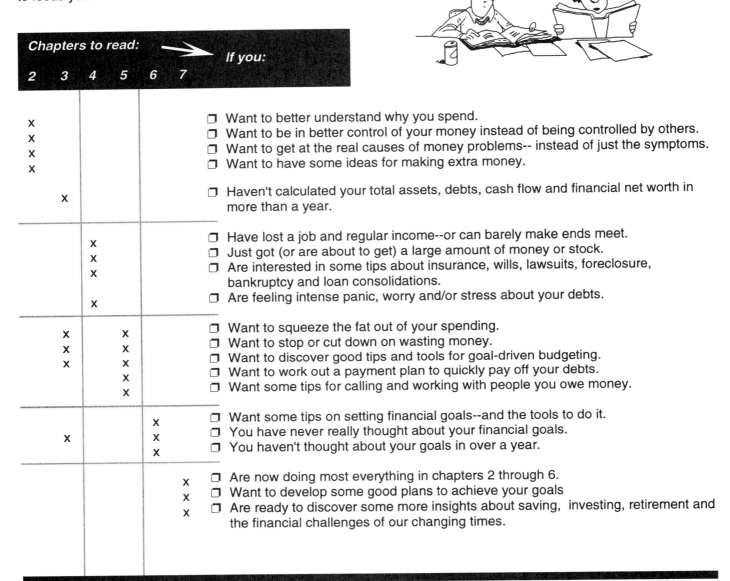

Chapters to read:						If you:
2	**3**	**4**	**5**	**6**	**7**	
X						❐ Want to better understand why you spend.
X						❐ Want to be in better control of your money instead of being controlled by others.
X						❐ Want to get at the real causes of money problems-- instead of just the symptoms.
X						❐ Want to have some ideas for making extra money.
	X					❐ Haven't calculated your total assets, debts, cash flow and financial net worth in more than a year.
		X				❐ Have lost a job and regular income--or can barely make ends meet.
		X				❐ Just got (or are about to get) a large amount of money or stock.
		X				❐ Are interested in some tips about insurance, wills, lawsuits, foreclosure, bankruptcy and loan consolidations.
		X				❐ Are feeling intense panic, worry and/or stress about your debts.
X			X			❐ Want to squeeze the fat out of your spending.
X			X			❐ Want to stop or cut down on wasting money.
X			X			❐ Want to discover good tips and tools for goal-driven budgeting.
			X			❐ Want to work out a payment plan to quickly pay off your debts.
			X			❐ Want some tips for calling and working with people you owe money.
				X		❐ Want some tips on setting financial goals--and the tools to do it.
X				X		❐ You have never really thought about your financial goals.
				X		❐ You haven't thought about your goals in over a year.
					X	❐ Are now doing most everything in chapters 2 through 6.
					X	❐ Want to develop some good plans to achieve your goals
					X	❐ Are ready to discover some more insights about saving, investing, retirement and the financial challenges of our changing times.

Use caution when tempted to skim a chapter or section. As hard as it may be, resist thinking that you know it all or don't need to read a chapter or section. At least read everything once.

Guaranteed, you'll be exposed to some tools and ideas that should improve your financial side of life and may make you laugh, think twice, change your life--or may even make you want to throw this workbook out.

Stick with us and keep an open mind. These ideas are working for many people. They should work for you too!

Chapter 2

The Psychology of Good and Bad Money Management

We can give you a few tips and tools to help you diagnose your financial situation and treat what appears to be a problem. But, would you be treating the real problem or just the tip of the iceberg?

If you just treat the symptoms of a problem, it's not long before it's back again. To get cured you must also attack the cause(s) of the problem. That's where this chapter comes in, and here's an overview of what's covered:

Part 1: Key Factors
> Ad wars and consumer propaganda.
> Knowledge and skills.
> Parents and other people.
> Era and experiences.
> Goals, dreams, obessions and experiences.

Part 2: What makes me throw money away?
> Ways of thinking and decision making.
> Other people.
> Interaction with spouse.
> Planning and other resources.
> Past ... as a kid.

Part 3: Recommendations for Greater Success
> Decide whether you want to be wealthy or rich, and why.
> Always decide why you want things.
> Defend yourself against deceptive ad wars.
> Build and maintain responsibility and integrity.
> Be wise about credit cards and their myths.
> Defend yourself against complusiveness and materialism.
> Be wise about the future.
> Choose friends carefully.
> Build your resources.
> Communicate and work with each other (a case study).
> Build family relationships.
> The past.
> Future generations.

Building Better Foundations

Part 1

Key Factors

We might have a number of bad habits to change, but what led us to the habits to begin with and what keeps us going? What deeper things must be addressed to help avoid the mistakes of the past? How can we better defend ourselves in the wars of inflation and consumer mania? Let's consider a few factors.

Ad Wars and Consumer Propaganda

We live in a society where there is a lot of consumer competition, marketing and propagandizing. Depending upon your reading, radio and TV habits, dozens to hundreds of messages come at you each day trying to get you to spend or invest your money on one thing or another.   The gimmicks used can be obvious or subtle. They may be sentimental, clever, funny, offensive, bizarre, or many other things. These messages come most obviously from ads. They also come from the examples and words of actors on TV and in the movies.

The name of the game has been "boost sales." For some companies, winning this game appears to be at all costs regardless of ethics or how the product might affect the person or society down the road! How have you been influenced by these messages?   Do you know how to be on guard against attacks?

Knowledge and Skills

Many people have never had basic money management education in their schooling or in workshops, to get them on the right track initially. What do you know? Where did you learn it? Are you applying what you know?

Parents and Other People

What did you learn about money from your parents, relatives, friends and other people in your life? Are you still learning from them? How do they influence you? What kind of examples, words of wisdom, encouragement and experiences have they provided?

Era & Experiences

What generation are you? Did you experience the depression? Did you ever hear first-hand stories about it from your parents, grandparents or other people who lived through it?   Have you thought seriously about the nuclear, terrorist and environmental threats? Have you lived in a family where the budget was ever tight, or where mom or dad lost a job--and it hit the family hard? How can living through these eras and experiences affect your way of managing money?

Goals, Dreams, Obsessions and Compulsions

How many of us have really thought about our goals and dreams? What are your six-month, one-year, five and ten-year goals? Are these your own goals and dreams? Or have you been sold a bill of goods by those around you and the ad wars? Are these worthy and realistic goals and aspirations? What will it take to get there?

The next two parts of this chapter can help you gain a few insights into how and why you manage your money.

❑   Part 2 includes a series of checklists probing the factors that can influence the way you manage money.

❑   Part 3 offers viewpoints and what might be agonizing recommendations to those who would be wise to fine-tune some areas of their lives.

These exercises may make some people feel uncomfortable, mad, depressed or downright hostile. So be it! We are in the business of helping people to grow and improve.

So, have courage, read on. Stick with this chapter to the last word. It may stir deep feelings and memories, yet you might also laugh!

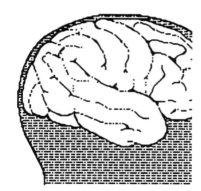

Part 2

What makes me throw money away?

The following checklist will give you an idea of some of the reasons why people get into financial trouble. Depending upon your situation, you may find any one or a number of these items as sources of your problem. Read each item carefully. Consider how you think about money, purchases and your financial lifestyle over the last two or three years.

First, evaluate how strongly you agree or disagree with each statement. Add up your score for each section, then determine the grand total and mark it on the diagram on page 19 to see where you currently stand regarding foundations for financial success.

	Strongly Agree			Strongly Disgree

A. *Ways of Thinking and Decision Making*

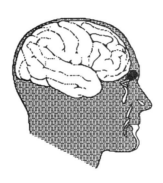

1. I feel as though I should have everything I want today (or as soon as possible). 1 2 3 4

2. The credit card companies wouldn't give me their cards if I didn't manage my money well. 1 2 3 4

3. If I want something, there's nothing wrong with renting, leasing or borrowing money to get it. 1 2 3 4

4. If it's broken, replace it. 1 2 3 4

5. I will feel better if I buy this or if I have this. 1 2 3 4

6. The credit card companies are just trying to help me out by sending me checks for cash advances, and it's very sensitive of the companies to send them around the Christmas holidays. 1 2 3 4

7. If only I made more money, everything would be better. 1 2 3 4

8. Never getting any nasty letters for being late on bills means I must be in pretty good financial shape. 1 2 3 4

9. I might as well use my credit cards since I have them. 1 2 3 4

10. If I pay the monthly minimum on my credit cards, I'm being a good money manager. 1 2 3 4

11. So what if I'm a little late paying bills. 1 2 3 4

12. The more I play the lotto or the long-shot gambles, the better my chances are of winning--big! 1 2 3 4

	Strongly Agree		Strongly Disagree
	•		•

13. I don't need to save for the future.   1 2 3 4
   (PS: And my answers to 14-17 explain why!)

    14.   That's what my pension, social security and   1 2 3 4
   other retirement benefits are for.

    15.   The world is going to end soon anyway, or I   1 2 3 4
   could die tomorrow.

    16.   Some white-collar criminals will rip me off   1 2 3 4
   anyway through some bank, pension, stock or
   real estate scheme.

    17.   I'm relying on the inheritance I get when my   1 2 3 4
   folks die or rich Auntie Em dies.

18. I should eat out less--but I wouldn't be saving that   1 2 3 4
   much when I figure in the time and expense it would
   take to fix these meals myself.

19. I really like what my neighbor (or other person) just   1 2 3 4
   got, and I need one, too.

20. Everyone else is wearing or getting one of these and I   1 2 3 4
   should too, or I'll be behind the times.

21. I must preserve my image at all costs even if it means   1 2 3 4
   spending more than I have. For example, even if I
   can't afford it, I might have to: buy some new clothes
   or shoes, buy a round of drinks for everyone, get a
   better looking car, tip big, go to expensive restaurants,
   get new toys for the kids, avoid generic products, etc.

22. What other people think of me (in terms of how I look,   1 2 3 4
   what I have, where and how I live) is more important
   than anything else.

23. I live for today and me. It's other people's job to worry   1 2 3 4
   about others and the future.

24. I buy with quality in mind. Money is no object.   1 2 3 4

25. I tend to be an impulse buyer. I purchase things   1 2 3 4
   whether I need them or not.

26. I tend to let other people talk me into buying things,   1 2 3 4
   even though it might go against my financial abilities
   and goals.

27. If I really need money, I'll just figure out a way to sue   1 2 3 4
   some wealthy company or person.

28. I deserve the very best. My parents, company and   1 2 3 4
   government owe it to me. I deserve whatever I want.

	Strongly Agree • 1 2	Strongly Disagree • 3 4
29. I enjoy flaunting what I have.	1 2	3 4
30. I am too good for certain jobs and tasks.	1 2	3 4
31. You've got to be willing to do some shady or risky things to make good money, or get the money you deserve.	1 2	3 4
32. Money means a lot to me. I spend a lot of time thinking about it.	1 2	3 4
33. The things I own mean a lot to me. I spend a lot of time thinking about them.	1 2	3 4

Section A Total = ☐

B. Other People

1. Most of my friends have very expensive taste in homes, decorating, clothing, possessions, lifestyle, etc.	1 2	3 4
2. Some of my friends drink quite a bit and/or use illegal drugs.	1 2	3 4
3. Many of the people I socialize with go out a lot to restaurants, bars, concerts, sports activities or do other things that usually require spending money.	1 2	3 4
4. Some of the people I associate with make fun of me, my clothes, where I live, what I do, or how I watch what I spend.	1 2	3 4
5. Many of the people I spend time with probably feel the same way I do about many of the items in sections A and C.	1 2	3 4
6. Many of the people I admire probably feel the same way I do about many of the items in sections A and C.	1 2	3 4

Section B Total = ☐

		Strongly Agree			Strongly Disagree
		• 1	2	3	• 4

C. Interaction with Spouse

Note: if you are not married, give yourself a 4 for each item in C.

1. As husband and wife we do not communicate about our finances.　　1 2 3 4

2. Neither of us knows what the other is spending money on.　　1 2 3 4

3. What I spend money on is none of his/her business.　　1 2 3 4

4. I bring home the bacon, so I say what we spend money on and who gets how much. And that's final!　　1 2 3 4

5. Neither of us checks with the other when we buy something over $75.　　1 2 3 4

6. I don't want my spouse to know anything about what I make or spend.　　1 2 3 4

7. My spouse wouldn't understand this financial stuff, even if I explained it.　　1 2 3 4

8. My spouse is in charge of the family finances and I trust her or him. To question decisions would hurt his or her feelings or cause bad feelings between us.　　1 2 3 4

Section C Total = ☐

D. Planning and Other Resources

1. I don't have a checking account to keep track of my expenses.　　1 2 3 4

2. I don't have a savings account.　　1 2 3 4

3. I have never thought about short, medium and long-term personal financial goals.　　1 2 3 4

4. I seldom shop for food from a comparative viewpoint.　　1 2 3 4

5. I rarely plan for my nonmonthly expenses such as birthdays, holidays, vacations, auto insurance, etc.　　1 2 3 4

6. I usually wait a fairly long time before submitting the forms needed to get reimbursed for business expenses.　　1 2 3 4

7. I buy or invest in things based on my feelings.　　1 2 3 4

8. I wait a fairly long time before submitting medical, dental and other bills that I can get reimbursed for.　　1 2 3 4

9. I have never set up a systematic "forced savings" as part of my normal day-to-day living.　　1 2 3 4

10. I have never done a detailed personal budget.　　1 2 3 4

		Strongly Agree			Strongly Disagree
		•			•
11.	I often forget to (or don't want to) meet the calling requirements of my medical plan.	1	2	3	4
12.	I have one or more credit cards and use them a lot.	1	2	3	4
13.	I often pay less than the full amount due on my credit cards.	1	2	3	4
14.	I spend more than one hour a day watching TV.	1	2	3	4

Section D Total = ☐

E. Past ... as a kid:

1.	My parents always gave me the money I needed and wanted.	1	2	3	4
2.	My parents and scholarships put me through college, and I didn't need a job or my own money to help.	1	2	3	4
3.	I was always allowed to spend whatever I made on anything I wanted. My parents never made me save any of my money.	1	2	3	4
4.	My parents never taught or shared with me their tips and principles of good money management.	1	2	3	4
5.	I always seemed to have more money than my friends.	1	2	3	4
6.	My parents regularly let me use one or more of their credit cards (gasoline, clothing store, etc.).	1	2	3	4
7.	I often complained if I couldn't get clothes, shoes or other things that were in vogue — trendy or fashionable things that other kids had.	1	2	3	4
8.	My parents nearly always gave in and bought me the things I talked them into.	1	2	3	4
9.	I have never actually been to a third world country (or poverty-struck neighborhood) and have never witnessed the poverty and life that a majority of people on earth experience.	1	2	3	4
10.	My parents always seemed to bail me out when I needed cash, needed my own car, or fell behind on loans.	1	2	3	4

		Strongly Agree			Strongly Disagree
11.	My parents always seemed to get whatever they wanted.	1	2	3	4
12.	My parents never encouraged me to give money to church or needy people.	1	2	3	4
13.	I don't remember my parents talking much about financial purchases, savings, goals or plans.	1	2	3	4

Section
E Total = [   ]

☞　Now tally up your scores from each section and plot the grand total below. Here are a few ways to interpret what your score means.

Grand
Total = [   ]

Total Points =	74	148	212	296
Foundations =	Very Sandy	Wet Sand	Sandstone	Solid Rock

Your Score

Now = _____

In 1 Year = _____

In 2 Years = _____

The sandier
your foundations, the
more your efforts to
improve your financial
situation will be exhausting.

It will also be easier
to blow your
money away.

Foundations
more like solid stone
can make: 1) Your climb
to greater wealth easier;
and 2) The longevity of your
wealth greater. The climb will
still take work, but you won't
fall down so much and you'll
have more energy to climb
higher — perhaps higher
than you ever
dreamed!

**Read on to see how you can strengthen your
foundations and keep them strong throughout life.**

Part 3

Recommendations for Greater Success

Now we get into the really tough reflective material. Your heart, conscience and soul may wrestle over some of these questions, but bear with it.

Few people may have ever had the foresight to confront you with the questions, views, and stances that you are about to read. Or, maybe they did, but you refused to listen. Both are probably more true if you were born after 1950 in which case you may be a victim of the decades of materialism and the "anything's OK" mentality driven by eroding values, morals and ethics.

Some of what we have said, and are about to say may irritate or annoy you. All we ask is that you think about these suggestions and viewpoints. Search your personality for the truth. Listen to your conscience.

Decide whether you want to be wealthy or rich, and why.

Richness has to do with the amount of money you will have in your life. Wealth has to do with the riches or treasures in your life — your quality of life.

If you want to be rich, you'll probably always be watching the stock market, valuing your possessions, calculating and recalculating your financial net worth and cash flow, looking for another deal, hot-tip or great long-shot, always examining the return on investment, and sacrificing everything and everyone else in your life--all for more money. You'll be focusing on what you can get out of people and life.

If you value wealth, you still may watch the numbers and be a good money manager, but you won't be obsessed. You'll also be appreciating and building relationships with the people in your life. You'll probably be more concerned about how you work with, and what you give to others and life, than what you get from them.

You'll build your relationships, knowledge and abilities not necessarily for the sake of money, but for the satisfaction and joy of growth and a higher quality of life. Making financial sacrifices will likely be easier for you.

What's more valuable to you, being rich or wealthy? What if you lost all your money and assets? How would you feel? What would be left? What would you do? Who would be left? Where would you turn? Who would stand by you if you had no money?

Tough questions! But the sooner you answer these, the more it can dramatically begin to affect your life and the lives of others in your life--for the better!

Always decide why you want things.

Some people want things to make them feel better. Others are buying because they believe that the product will improve their sex life, help them make friends, be more sophisticated, look better — basically be a happier, more accepted and worthy person.

These messages may come through ads and TV shows verbally, visually and subliminally.

Who's ripe for these deceptions:

- ❏ People who don't know or care what they value, believe, need or want.

- ❏ People with low self-esteem.

- ❏ People who want more pleasure or power, fewer wrinkles, better sex, to be cool, or to look better.

- ❏ People who make decisions based on feelings and moods.

- ❏ People who have a void in their life.

- ❏ Children (from 1-21 years).

Yet, the product will run out. Fashions will change. What's cool will change. The better feeling will only last for a little while. Does this all happen by chance?

You'll either have to buy more or switch to get back on track. This almost sounds like an addiction. Or it sounds like a sick relationship, where someone is playing manipulative mind games with you based on your weaknesses and needs.

Fortunately not all companies are like this. Many strive to meet genuine needs and worthy wants with quality products and services. They also use ethical advertising practices and avoid the use of persuasive communications with children and other vulnerable people in our society.

Traits of Solid People

Some people have a little more self-esteem and are less vulnerable. Below are some of the traits of these people. Use the assessment to the right to rank yourself on these traits.

I am making positive moves in this direction.

	Strongly Disagree			Strongly Agree

❏ I know who I am and have a strong sense of purpose.

1 2 3 4

❏ I know what I value, believe, and want.

1 2 3 4

❏ I know the difference between wants and needs.

1 2 3 4

❏ I can spot a lie and a "con" quickly.

1 2 3 4

❏ I have really thought life through and reflect upon it regularly.

1 2 3 4

❏ I make decisions considering goals, vision, values and beliefs.

1 2 3 4

❏ I am developing discipline, resources, abilities and efforts to do what it takes to meet true needs and reach my goals and dreams.

1 2 3 4

❏ I want to improve my self-esteem and be smarter about money. I really want it and am willing to work at it--no matter how I feel. It is a goal.

1 2 3 4

Reading this workbook is a great start.

Defend Yourself Against Manipulative Advertising

You can control how many manipulative ads you are exposed to in very simple ways. Here's how:

	I already do this.	*I will do this starting:* *Now* or *Date*
❏ Watch less TV.	Yes	Now _____
❏ Listen to radio stations with fewer ads.	Yes	Now _____
❏ Shift your watching and listening to shows that are more educational.	Yes	Now _____
❏ Mute the sound during a commercial.	Yes	Now _____
❏ Don't spend so much time reading the product catalogs mailed to you.	Yes	Now _____
❏ Evaluate and look for the motives and manipulations in ads, commercials and catalogs you are exposed to.	Yes	Now _____

		I already do this.	I will do this starting: Now or Date
❏	Take action against the lies and manipulations by not buying the product. You can write to the company, too!	Yes	Now _____
❏	Do things to build up your self-esteem and the esteem of others in your life.	Yes	Now _____
❏	Do some soul searching about what you believe in, value and what your advertising ethics are or would be.	Yes	Now _____
❏	Know the differences between needs, wants and temptations. Know what you really need and what's good for you. Compare this with what you may want or be tempted to want. Keep this in mind when you see ads and shows.	Yes	Now _____
❏	If they have "buy me this" tantrums, don't take the kids with you when you go shopping.	Yes	Now _____
❏	Don't forget to help your kids with all of this.	Yes	Now _____
❏	Have fun with all of this in conversations with family and friends.	Yes	Now _____

Try this all for a few weeks. Then, apply it for life! You won't regret it.

Build and Maintain Responsibility and Integrity

And, there are those who don't care if they are consistently late in paying bills or not paying at all. They say they will do things, but don't. Then they make excuses. Unfortunately, this, too, can be strongly linked to: an absence of values or very questionable ones, and/or a lack of direction and vision.

Creditors and landlords can't be blamed for their reaction to laggards who don't care about their responsibilities. Send notes. Take legal action. Repossess. Kick them out. Garnish wages. Put liens on accounts. And let others know about the bad financial attitudes and habits via the credit history and credit tracking organizations.

The trouble is that these penalties don't always result in the person changing. It might help to put this type of person through a money management course, but only if they truly want to change and become a better money manager.

Be Wise About Credit Cards

By themselves, most credit cards are not the problem. The ones that are bad are those that start charging interest as soon as you purchase something (versus those that charge interest if you don't pay your bill on time in full). Like alcohol, it's how you abuse credit cards that causes problems.

Some people have never really had a problem with credit cards. First of all, they've got the right kind of credit cards with low annual percentage rates and interest charged after a grace period. Second, they don't abuse them. Sure, once in a while they may pay less than the full amount due, but not often and when they do, they squirm.

On the other hand, some people have problems with credit cards from the day they first get them. They consider their credit limit to be cash in the bank, to be used for anything they want. They feel the more cards they have the more cash on hand--the more spending power available. Like the alcoholic, these people are spendaholics. The presence of any credit card tempts them, and it is a very tough temptation to resist.

Worse yet are the friendly "we care about you at this special time of financial need" letters that offer you checks for cash advances to buy Christmas presents.

All of this is why people who have credit card problems should get all their cards together and cut them up, just as the recovering alcoholic must get rid of any alcohol in the house. It makes the recovery much easier.

Credit Card Myths

Finally, there are a number of myths about credit cards that need to be cleared up.

1) The credit card companies would prefer that you pay the minimum monthly amount. By not paying the full amount they can charge you outrageous interest on the balance you owe and make money on your ignorance.

2) You are not being a great money manager if you pay the minimum monthly amount due. However, you are being responsible regarding your credit card obligation to pay what you owe.

   But, you are throwing your own hard-earned money down the drain on the interest they will charge you. This may be unwise regarding your current and future financial well-being.

   You can outsmart your credit cards by doing the following:

   ❏   Use them sparingly, if at all; then
   ❏   Pay the bill in full--on time, every time!

3) No, the credit card companies are not being sensitive to your needs by sending you checks for cash advances around Christmas time. In fact, they are exploiting the ignorant and foolish around the time they are more vulnerable to temptations of spending and needing easy cash.

   ❏   Do yourself a favor and rip them up!

4) Very few banks or firms will take back their credit card if you don't use it.

5) Beware of special colored prestigious credit cards that give you "special" privileges or insurance. The fees may be two to four times higher than the usual fee for a regular card. These cards are geared for those who have the lifestyles of the rich and famous (whether they can afford it or not).

Defend Yourself Against Compulsiveness, Materialism and a Big Ego

People who think the world revolves around them are tough to get through to. They think everyone owes them something — jobs, money, sex, gifts, compliments, and insulation from criticism. They often think they are too good for certain jobs.

Usually, the only hope of changing these characters is an upsetting event that brings the harsh realities of life into focus — a close encounter with death or a significant loss of income with a dramatic downturn in lifestyle--something like what happened in the movie "Trading Places." Even then, there are no guarantees. A person may not change or the change may not last.

Where are you now?

There is much more hope regarding prevention. Consider these strategies:

	I already do this.	I will do this starting: Now or Date
☐ Do your best to stay in touch with the tragedies and quality of life of others who may be less fortunate than you.	Yes	Now _____
☐ Regularly visit and help your aging relatives and friends.	Yes	Now _____
☐ Volunteer for causes that help those in need. Help when tragedy strikes a person, family or community.	Yes	Now _____
☐ Get involved in short or long-term missions or volunteer work through your church, Red Cross, Peace Corps or many other charitable organizations--locally and overseas.	Yes	Now _____

These experiences can be very humbling and can enhance your views and appreciation for life.

Be Wise About the Future

Some people are very pessimistic about the future. Chances are that it is not those who are worried about the future that have money problems. Rather, it's those who are cavalier about the future.

In other words, people who use their outlook on the future as an excuse for spending or not saving are the ones who have problems.

	I already do this.	*I will do this starting: Now or Date*
❐ Many people are sincerely concerned about the future. These concerns (including some pessimism, or is it realism) actually become powerful motivators to manage money and other areas of life better. What if I lose my job? What if the country goes into a recession? What if social security or pension benefits are not adequate when I retire? What if war breaks out? What if one of us dies before our time?	Yes	Now _____
❐ Seriousness about these concerns motivates the wise people to action which is partly reflected in the way they manage and save their money.	Yes	Now _____

Choose Friends Carefully

Peer pressure did not stop in high school. The pressures people can put on you are often subtle, sometimes obvious and always very powerful.

❐ Regularly evaluate the friends you have and the company you keep.	Yes	Now _____

Some people will lure you down into their own paths of foolishness, lack of values or ethics. They will do it through flaunting, ridicule, snubbing their noses at you, fast-talking or other ways to manipulate your feelings and ego.

Other people are really your friends and will help you to grow. True friends will challenge your foolish ways, and risk jeopardizing the relationship by speaking the truth. Most good friends will try to do this in a firm, yet caring way.

❐ Unless you are on a mission to help people or enforce the law, avoid spending a lot of time with people you think are fools regarding money, alcohol, drugs and life in general. You've got to be pretty strong in your values, beliefs, will and mission not to get dragged down with these folks.	Yes	Now _____
❐ Also, until you know who you are and are strong in your own values and ethics, avoid those you believe have questionable values or questionable ethics regarding making or spending money, and life in general.	Yes	Now _____
❐ Begin looking for people you consider to be wise (versus rich). Look for them at work, church, in your family and community. Chances are they are wise at managing their money as well. Watch them. Ask them to share what they think are wise money management tips. Ask them to encourage you.	Yes	Now _____
❐ Make your friends wise ones. Have frequent contact with them.	Yes	Now _____

		I already do this.	I will do this starting: Now or Date

Build Your Resources

Get your hidden money out of your safe, laundry basket, shoe box or from under your bed.

❐ At the very least, put your money into a bank.   Yes   Now _____

At home, your money is not working for you. In fact, it will depreciate. Put it in a bank or elsewhere where you can earn interest.

❐ Get a checking account.   Yes   Now _____

❐ Be sure to enter every check and deposit in the register.   Yes   Now _____

❐ Balance your checkbook every month.   Yes   Now _____

❐ No matter how in debt or tight things are financially, start at least one forced savings plan even if it is $25-$50 a month. Consider this amount like a mortgage or rent. Force yourself to pay your savings or money market account each week or month.   Yes   Now _____

❐ You may be able to make this easier by having your employer or bank deposit this amount electronically to an account at a certain time each month.   Yes   Now _____

See your human resources department and bank for details.

❐ As you pay off debts or earn more money, increase the amount you are saving and investing.   Yes   Now _____

Interaction with Spouse... loaded gun, hot-potato...

This is a tough thing to write about because so many marriages and the people within them are different. But, I'll (Bob Gorsky) take a shot at it using a personal example.

Challenges & Adjustments

It is very easy for me to spend money. However, my wife is very frugal regarding money matters. One day I came back from my ritual visit to the hardware store with a brand new shop-vac. It was on sale for just under $100. When I got home, I began to take it out of the box and then...my wife saw it.

She went through the roof! She said "How could you buy this now?" I said I had thought it all through and it made sense to buy ... that "we" really needed it. I felt like I did something logical; however, she seemed irritated with me for days.

Sharing Thoughts & Decisions

Finally, we got to talking and <u>hearing</u> one another. She felt that we did not talk about things before I made decisions. I rarely asked her opinion, or talked about it together before I made even moderate purchases.

So, we agreed that we would consult one another before buying any non-grocery purchase over $75. It isn't easy, but I've been doing my best to abide by this.

The Test

Then one day, I was at the hardware store again searching for some obscure bolt, when I saw something else I thought we needed. It was on sale, too! I picked it up and began walking to the cashier.

Conscience

As I waited in line, I got this haunting feeling about my commitment to change. So I got on the phone and called my wife. We talked about some sensible considerations and agreed it was a good thing to get at this time.

Feedback

When I came home, she was glowing and said it really made her feel good that I called.

Team

We still talk about purchases ahead of time. And, it seems we talk about more things, sharing thoughts and thinking decisions through together, as opposed to independently. We have become a team, working together more and more. It didn't happen over night. It happens little by little.

Why?

So what does all this mean? Why am I sharing all this with you? From a marriage and money perspective, the nuts and bolts of it all is on the next page.

		We already do this.	We will do this starting: Now or Date
		Where are you now?	

Marriage Partnership

		We already do this.	We will do this starting: Now or Date
❐	Realize that one might work outside the home to make money but the other is working at home to save it. Value both of these contributions.	Yes	Now _____
❐	Avoid using money as a measure of who is worth more in the family ("I make the money so I have the power.").	Yes	Now _____
❐	Frequently acknowledge each other's contributions, earnings, and support.	Yes	Now _____
❐	Share more and decide together--about money matters, kids and the many other areas of life.	Yes	Now _____
❐	Trust each other more and don't let each other down.	Yes	Now _____
❐	Ignore your ego.	Yes	Now _____
❐	Do your best to build each other's self-esteem and the relationship you have together.	Yes	Now _____

We could go on, but this is not a marriage enrichment book. From a financial perspective, the main point is this: If you communicate better and manage your money better, your marriage will be better.

❐	Get some help if you've got a bad marriage — if one is a spendaholic, alcoholic, gambler, or drug user. Contact your employee assistance program, church, mental health agency, personal or marriage counselor for advice and support.	Yes	Now _____

Not getting help can result in money and other problems that only get worse.

New Marriages

Before you get married:

1)	Share goals and dreams (money related and other);	Yes	Now _____
2)	Share money management philosophies, ideas and practices;	Yes	Now _____
3)	Watch and compare actions with words;	Yes	Now _____
4)	If it's your second marriage and you have an estate, see a lawyer.	Yes	Now _____

All of these may help you to avoid or minimize potential problems later.

		Where are you now?	
		I already do this.	*I will do this starting: Now or Date*

The Past

Realistically, you can't change how you were brought up regarding money. But you might be able to make up for the discussions you never had with your folks.

❏ If you think they are pretty good money managers and you are on good speaking terms with them, ask your parents to share their words of wisdom regarding money matters.   Yes   Now _____

❏ If your grandparents are still alive try it with them, too. Listen to what they have to say.   Yes   Now _____

❏ Take notes if necessary.   Yes   Now _____

❏ Ask them to share the advice for the future generations. Do it on video and make it fun!   Yes   Now _____

Remember, it's their opinion, so you can take it or leave it. But it will be a nice gesture and they may offer some worthwhile advice.

Future Generations

Are you passing your strengths onto your children? You have a chance to reverse the negative cycles and continue the positive.

❏ You can't change your past, but search category E (page 18) for some ideas to avoid similar mistakes with your children.   Yes   Now _____

❏ Allowances, weekly chores, odd jobs, a savings account, checking account, help in paying the household bills, responsibility for certain purchases, giving to and helping others--these are a few of the opportunities available to build good money management skills.   Yes   Now _____

❏ Put yourself on video for your kids and their kids. Offer words of wisdom and encourage them to be wise in their lives.   Yes   Now _____

❏ Before your daughter/son leaves for college (or to live on their own), work with them to develop a budget and financial plan. Give them a copy of this book. Encourage them to read it and use the tools (inside) for managing their money wisely and making their dreams come true.

Parents have the above (and many other opportunities) to inspire their kids toward wise money management.

Notes

Chapter 3

Assessing your financial status and operations.

In chapter 1 we suggested that you run your personal financial life like a business--with you as the president!

Good presidents have a good grip on what's going on in the many different departments of their business. Do you? How aware are you of your financial operations?

This chapter contains the following critical tools that you will need to assess where you are financially:

Exercise

3.1	Adding your assets.
3.2	Adding your debts.
3.3	Determining financial net worth.
3.4	Sources of monthly income.
3.5	Regular expenses.
3.6	Determining cash flow.

The insights discovered will be critical for rebuilding or fine-tuning your financial operations. What can result are stronger foundations for lasting financial prosperity.

Every successful business, whether large or small, must work with these same tools to survive.

You won't regret taking the time to complete these exercises. You'll gain many insights. You will also need the information for other parts of this workbook.

Where are you now ?

Assets

The first step in determining where you are financially is to list all of your assets. The simplest definition of an asset is anything you own that is worth money.

Liquid assets include cash <u>and</u> anything that can be converted into cash within ten days.

Non-liquid investments, such as your residence or some employer-sponsored savings and stock plans, take longer. This is important to know if you are considering selling or liquidating some of your assets to pay off some debts.

Instructions

The top section of the form for exercise 3.1 is for liquid assets and the bottom is for non-liquid assets.

Although there are many items listed in exercise 3.1, you may currently have only two or three. Don't let this discourage you. There is a column for your situation right now. The other two columns are to be filled out one and two years from now.

If you apply the guidelines offered in this booklet, you should see your total assets increase from one year to the next. Each year, fill in the figures requested. Then, make a note on a separate list to come back to this exercise at the next tax return time. You will be going through your financial records then and can determine your progress.

There is an easy way to determine the value of your assets. Look at each line in exercise 3.1 and estimate what you would get if you sold that asset today. You may have to guess at some items, such as the value of your household furnishings, automobile and other personal property.

Be careful not to overvalue things that may have a special value only to you. This might include items such as portraits of family members or family hand-me-downs.

To get the value of savings bonds, you should obtain a listing from your local bank, savings and loan or credit union, which can tell you the exact value of those bonds. If you have a life insurance policy with a cash value, call your agent and get the value if you were to cash the policy in right now. If you have a personal residence, you can call a local real estate agent and get a rough estimate of the value. To estimate the value of your car, you can get the "Blue Book" value from the Internet or your bank.

Exercise 3.1:   Adding Up Your Assets

Value

	Now	In 1 year	In 2 years
A. Liquid Assets			

- Checking accounts
- Savings accounts
- Cash (under matress, in shoe box, wallet)
- Savings bonds
- Money market funds
- Credit union funds
- Money owed to you
- Life insurance (cash values)
- Other investments (mutual funds, etc.)

_____

_____

_____

- Other liquid assets

_____

_____

_____

Total liquid assets ➔   = _____   = _____   = _____

B. Nonliquid Assets

Not Retirement Specific
- Personal residence
- Other land and real estate
- Money owed to you
- Personal property
- Household furnishings
- Automobile(s)
- Other

Retirement Specific (Tax-Deferred)
- IRA (personal and company)
- Company 401(k)/Retirement Savings Plan
- Other: _____
- Other: _____

Total nonliquid assets ➔   = _____   = _____   = _____

C. Total Assets (A+B) ➔   = _____   = _____   = _____

Debts

The simplest way to determine the amounts for exercise 3.2, is to look at every debt and determine how much you would need to pay it off right now. To determine the amount for your credit cards and charge accounts, simply use the figure from your most recent statement. For items such as car loans or other installment loans, you will have to call the lender and ask how much you would owe if you paid it off today.

Although you may have a long list of debts for this exercise, do not let that scare you. We will show you how to eliminate these one at a time. Here's how to do the next exercise.

Instructions

The goal of this exercise is to know all your debts now and then be able to watch the amount decrease from one year to the next.

In the first column, simply fill in the amounts owed for each of the items listed. Once again, there is a column for your situation now and columns for one and two years down the road. Make a note on your "TO-DO" list to do this exercise again at tax time.

Determining Your
Financial Net Worth

You can now compare the value of your assets and the amount of the debts by listing the bottom line from exercises 3.1 and 3.2.

Instructions

If your total assets are more than your total debts, then you want to focus on increasing that excess every year. If your total debts are more than your assets, you will need to carefully work with the upcoming worksheets and tips on income and expenses to help turn that situation around.

If, on paper, your assets are more than your liabilities, congratulations ... but, don't rest easy! Consider your short-term, intermediate and long-term goals. You may not have the right mix of assets for achieving your goals when examining the current status of the economy, liquidity of your assets and other important factors. This is also known as being "asset rich and cash poor."

Exercise 3.2: Adding Your Debts	Amount Owed		
Description	*Now*	*In 1 year*	*In 2 years*
Master Card/Visa			
_____	_____	_____	_____
_____	_____	_____	_____
Other credit cards and charge accounts			
_____	_____	_____	_____
_____	_____	_____	_____
_____	_____	_____	_____
_____	_____	_____	_____
_____	_____	_____	_____
Car loans			
_____	_____	_____	_____
_____	_____	_____	_____
Utilities			
_____	_____	_____	_____
_____	_____	_____	_____
Home: mortgage and equity loans			
_____	_____	_____	_____
_____	_____	_____	_____
Loans from family and friends			
_____	_____	_____	_____
_____	_____	_____	_____
_____	_____	_____	_____
Gambling debts/loans			
_____	_____	_____	_____
_____	_____	_____	_____
Other (education, medical, etc.)			
_____	_____	_____	_____
_____	_____	_____	_____
Total Debts →	=_____	=_____	=_____

Exercise 3.3 Financial Net Worth			
	Now	*In 1 Year*	*In 2 Years*
A. Total Assets (Line C from exercise 3.1)	_____	_____	_____
B. Total Debts (Total from exercise 3.2)	-_____	-_____	-_____
C. Financial Net Worth (A-B) →	=_____	=_____	=_____

Ideally, financial net worth should increase with each passing year.
✍ *Do exercises 3.1, 3.2 and 3.3 each year at tax return time.*

Adding Income	Although paychecks may be weekly or every two weeks, it is easier to look at incomes and expenses on a monthly basis. Many expenses are paid on a monthly basis so it makes it easier to match up your total incomes and expenses.
	Exercise 3.4 on the next page starts with your gross salary and shows withholdings for taxes and other payroll deductions. The reason for showing the deductions is that you may currently have money withheld for various employer savings programs. You may want to temporarily reduce or stop the withholding and use the money to reduce some debt.
	If you or your spouse receives extra income from overtime or part-time jobs, you should use low or conservative estimates of these amounts because they may change. If you plan on having the money coming in and it doesn't, it can throw off your payment or savings plan.
	How many sources of income you have depends on your situation including age, work history, employee benefits, investments and more.
Instructions	Complete this exercise to get an idea of your income. You can find most of the information on your paycheck stub(s), monthly statements from your bank and investment funds, checkbook register and your tax return.
	Fill in these figures either starting with the gross salary and showing the deductions, or simply fill in the Net Salary lines. Although this page has many sources of income, most individuals will have only a few.

Exercise 3.4:　Sources of Monthly Income

Monthly Income Generated:

		By Me	By Spouse
Salary Income	Gross salary		
	Job 1	_____	_____
	Job 2	_____	_____
	Minus taxes		
	Federal	_____	_____
	State	_____	_____
	Social security	_____	_____
	Minus other payroll deductions		
	Savings: _____	_____	_____
	Savings: _____	_____	_____
	Insurance (health, life, etc.)	_____	_____
	United Way	_____	_____
	Other: _____	_____	_____
	Net salary income →	_____	_____

		By me	By spouse	Jointly
Other Income	Interest	_____	_____	_____
	Dividends	_____	_____	_____
	Capital gains (stock sales)	_____	_____	_____
	Rents	_____	_____	_____
	Profit from business	_____	_____	_____
	Pension	_____	_____	_____
	Disability	_____	_____	_____
	Unemployment	_____	_____	_____
	Alimony	_____	_____	_____
	Child support	_____	_____	_____
	Social security	_____	_____	_____
	Reimbursements			
	Medical insurance	_____	_____	_____
	Auto insurance	_____	_____	_____
	Business expenses	_____	_____	_____
	Misc. income _____	_____	_____	_____
	Total other income →	_____	_____	_____

Spendable Income	Net salary income	+_____	+_____	
	Total other income	+_____	+_____	+_____
	Total spendable income →	M=_____	S=_____	J=_____
	Grand total spendable income →	M + S + J = _____		

Adding Up
Regular Expenses

Instructions

Whether you realize it or not, you shape your spending around your situation and goals. Lose a job and you cut down spending. Get a raise and you are tempted to spend the gain. Retire and your budget adjusts.

Remember, the real power of budgeting comes in as you increase your awareness of what you spend and begin to make planned changes to achieve certain goals. But before we get into tips on how to adjust your spending and conserve or build your savings, we suggest you look at where your money is going now. Then, try to anticipate how it could change for goals you have now, for "tight times" and retirement.

First, let's take a look at your average monthly spending. This can be fearful, shocking, depressing or not surprising at all depending upon how much you stay on top of your spending lifestyle. Regardless of how you might feel, do this exercise. Your efforts will generate insights that may result in many money management ideas.

In this exercise, regular expenses are broken into many typical areas and subcategories. In listing these dollar amounts, you will have to go back to all of the following records:

√ Checkbook (if you have one)
√ Credit card statements
√ Cash receipts (if you've been keeping them)
√ Your memory

Consider all these sources when you estimate your current monthly averages for each expense area. If you don't have a checkbook and monthly credit card statements, you will need to check cash receipts <u>and</u> think back and guess the amounts. Look at the most recent four-week period and try to remember how much you spent on food, gas, and other items. Then project that on a monthly basis.

The important thing to remember is to be honest and realistic about these figures. Later we will indicate how you can review the variable expenses to determine how you might be able to save a few extra dollars in each category. You'll be amazed at how small amounts can add up quickly.

Estimate these amounts as accurately and honestly as possible. Some expenses are tough to plan for because they are not monthly or vary from month to month. It is critical to plan for these because they are the ones that usually are not saved for. These will include items such as birthday and other gifts, utilities, repairs, holidays, certain insurance payments and vacations. Simply total these expenses over a full 12-month period of time. Divide the total for each amount by 12 for the monthly average. For the credit cards and other loans, show the minimum amount required to be paid or actual amount you pay, whichever is greater.

Meanwhile, go through column 1 and determine which you could eliminate or reduce in the event of a job loss or a lot of debts. Record these answers in the tight-times conservation column 2. You can use columns 3 and 4 to develop revised (or estimated) budgets to save more for various goals and for retirement.

Chapters 4 and 5 offer tips for reducing specific expenses.

Exercise 3.5: Regular Expenses	Current Monthly Average	Tight-Times Conservation Budget	Goal-Driven Savings Budget	Retirement Budget
Expense Areas				

Residence					
	Mortgage/Rent	$_____	$_____	$_____	$_____
	Property Taxes (if not included in mortgage)	$_____	$_____	$_____	$_____
	Repairs and Maintenance	$_____	$_____	$_____	$_____
	Improvements and Decorating	$_____	$_____	$_____	$_____
Utilities	Gas	$_____	$_____	$_____	$_____
	Electric	$_____	$_____	$_____	$_____
	Phone: Home, Mobile, Pager & Other	$_____	$_____	$_____	$_____
	City: Sewer, Water & Garbage	$_____	$_____	$_____	$_____
Insurance	Life and Disability	$_____	$_____	$_____	$_____
	Health: Medical, Dental, Rx, Vision	$_____	$_____	$_____	$_____
	Auto	$_____	$_____	$_____	$_____
	Homeowners and Property	$_____	$_____	$_____	$_____
Loan Payments	Equity Loan	$_____	$_____	$_____	$_____
	Auto Loan(s)	$_____	$_____	$_____	$_____
	Credit Card(s)	$_____	$_____	$_____	$_____
	Student Loan(s)	$_____	$_____	$_____	$_____
	Other Loans	$_____	$_____	$_____	$_____
Food	Groceries	$_____	$_____	$_____	$_____
	Eating Out, Treats, Coffee, Soda, etc.	$_____	$_____	$_____	$_____
Clothing: work, social, play and sports		$_____	$_____	$_____	$_____
Health: all reimbursed and non-reimbursed bills		$_____	$_____	$_____	$_____
Retirement Savings (not listed in exercise 3.4)		$_____	$_____	$_____	$_____
Other Non-Retirement Savings (not listed in exercise 3.4)		$_____	$_____	$_____	$_____
Business Related Expenses: including those reimbursed		$_____	$_____	$_____	$_____
Travel	Auto: Gas	$_____	$_____	$_____	$_____
	Auto: Maintenance and Repairs	$_____	$_____	$_____	$_____
	Fares: Train, Bus, Air, Cab, etc.	$_____	$_____	$_____	$_____
Education	Newspapers and Publications	$_____	$_____	$_____	$_____
	Books, Tapes, Computer (HW/SW), Internet	$_____	$_____	$_____	$_____
	Tuition and Fees	$_____	$_____	$_____	$_____
Contributions	Churches, Synagogues, Other Faith Groups	$_____	$_____	$_____	$_____
	Charities, Scouts and Other Causes	$_____	$_____	$_____	$_____
Recreation	Holidays, Vacations, Camps and Get-Aways	$_____	$_____	$_____	$_____
	Pool, Y, Health Club, Golf and Other Fees	$_____	$_____	$_____	$_____
	Museums, Zoos and Other Cultural Activities	$_____	$_____	$_____	$_____
	Events (sports, concerts, movies)	$_____	$_____	$_____	$_____
	Videos, CDs, Tapes and Electronic Games	$_____	$_____	$_____	$_____
	Photos and Hobbies (equipment & supplies)	$_____	$_____	$_____	$_____
	Cable or Satellite TV	$_____	$_____	$_____	$_____
	Other Equip. and Fees (sports, camping)	$_____	$_____	$_____	$_____
Miscellaneous	Child Care, Allowances	$_____	$_____	$_____	$_____
	Hair and Cosmetics	$_____	$_____	$_____	$_____
	Legal, Accounting & Other Prof'l Fees	$_____	$_____	$_____	$_____
	Appliances, Furniture and Tools	$_____	$_____	$_____	$_____
	Alimony &/or Child Support	$_____	$_____	$_____	$_____
	Gifts, Games and Toys (not listed above)	$_____	$_____	$_____	$_____
	Alcohol, Tobacco, Drugs and/or Bars	$_____	$_____	$_____	$_____
	Lottos, Racetracks and Other Gambling	$_____	$_____	$_____	$_____
	Tickets, Fines and Bail	$_____	$_____	$_____	$_____
	Cash Unknown	$_____	$_____	$_____	$_____
	Other _____	$_____	$_____	$_____	$_____

TOTALS → $_____ $_____ $_____ $_____

Now, it's time to compare your total spendable income with your total expenses from the previous two exercises.

Exercise 3.6 : **Determining Cash Flow**	Spendable Income (grand total) _____ from exercise #3.4 Total Current Expenses — _____ from exercise #3.5 Net Cash Flow = _____ see +/- key below *If + = Extra cash to save, invest or spend.* *If - = Amount you're spending more than you're making.*

What Cash Flow Means

Your net cash flow is the money that is available to either reduce your debts or to save for your goals or it's the amount you are overspending, beyond your regular income.

Tight? Next steps.

If you are spending more than what you bring in, then it is critical that you review every line in exercise 3.5 to determine how you can squeeze out some additional dollars. Use column 2 (conservation) to evaluate each expense area. In general, determine whether or not it's a necessity (can you live a decent life without it?). Then, determine whether or not you might be able to change the amount you're spending in each area.

Finally, consider how much you can squeeze out of each area for important goals. In column 3, fill in a new (reduced) target goal of spending for the areas that your conscience tells you to reduce. This may result in a bit of healthy anxiety. Have courage, it may result in some wonderful things! Later you'll discover how you can put this money to work to achieve your goals quicker than you thought you could.

Reimbursable Expenses

Get 'em In Quick!

You should also consider other situations that may cause your cash-in to be less than your cash-out. One may be when you pay business or medical expenses but don't get reimbursed until a later time. If you must fill out reports or forms to get reimbursed, make sure you do it as quickly as possible. This may also apply to certain dental and educational expenses that you have to pay for up-front and get reimbursed for later.

Stay Tuned

The checklists in the next chapters will help you study your expenses to determine where you can save additional dollars for your short, medium, and long-term goals.

Chapter 4
Situations Requiring a Clear Head

Review these pages of this section if you:

Think Twice !!!!

Skip the items that don't apply ... and move on to the next chapter!
Also, consider sharing this chapter with a friend in need.

Income and Job

Have lost (or may soon lose) a job or income due to layoff, injury or disability, nonpayment of alimony or child support, etc.

☐ Determine financial needs for next 12+ months. Chapter 5 can help you to do a detailed expense projection and see ways to reduce expenses.

☐ Assess sources of income and useable assets using the exercises in chapter 3 and considering the following:

○ If you lose a job, apply for unemployment compensation immediately because it is not retroactive if you wait a few weeks or months. This will decrease or cease when you begin to earn income again through a part- or full-time job. In the meantime, it will provide you with some income to meet basic living expenses.

○ If you have a job-related injury and disability, check with the state office of workman's (or worker's) compensation. Your human resources department may also be a source of information regarding procedures and contacts to begin the process of obtaining workman's compensation.

○ If it's not a job-related disability, check any personal disability insurance policies you may have.

○ If you have a major injury (amputations or loss of vision) also check any company sponsored and personal accidental death and disability insurance coverages.

☐ Determine which assets can be liquidated and turned into cash if necessary (e.g. IRAs, mutual funds, etc.).

☐ Check with an accountant, enrolled agent or tax attorney to determine the tax consequences of liquidating assets.

☐ Go into a financial conservation mode!

Immediately cut unnecessary expenses and purchases. Use the rest of this chapter and chapter 5 for ideas and immediate actions you can take.

❏ If child support or alimony is late or unpaid, call your ex-spouse in an attempt to resolve the problem. If you are not on speaking terms or the problem is not being resolved through personal efforts, then contact your lawyer for next steps.

❏ Begin exploring new job options.

　　○ Consider looking for part-time employment to generate some cash. Options may be: temporary employment agencies, subcontracting, consulting projects, substitute teaching, seasonal jobs (e.g. working in a clothing store around Christmas time) and many other alternatives.

　　○ Take advantage of any available outplacement services such as: developing a resume, developing interview skills, job searches and retraining.

　　○ Determine how long employer-sponsored insurances and benefits will last, the cost to you and when and which of these need to be replaced and then paid for by you. *Under COBRA regulations, employees with company-sponsored health benefits may choose to continue them (at cost plus a small administrative fee) for up to 18 months after employment ceases. The cost of this coverage may be well below other options since you are getting access to the company's group rates. See your human resources department for more information.*

　　○ Consider a new career--something you always wanted to do. Do your homework and consider your current skills and the training you may need to accomplish this goal. Go for it!

❏ Strive to make lemonade out of lemons. Many apparently dismal situations can turn into fortunate opportunities that result in refreshing changes and enhancements in career and family life.

❏ Strive to stay positive. Stay away from people with a sour grapes attitude. Focus on the things to be thankful for. Be wise and resourceful in where you seek your advice, encouragement, and inner strength.

Big Money!

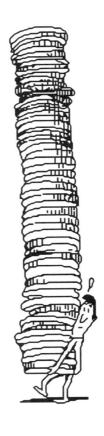

Just received a fairly large sum of money (via an inheritance, winning the lotto, ESOP, 401(k) distribution, job severence package, life insurance settlement/payout, etc.).

❏ Don't go on a spending binge blowing it all on foolish things.

❏ Consider the value of using it to pay off or pay down some debts.

❏ Consider safer income generating investments (remember, $100,000 at just 5% per year generated $5,000 of annual interest). See chapter 7 for tips and ideas regarding investment safety.

❏ Put a good portion of it away for retirement.

❏ Watch out for the calls from investment brokers who "care" about your financial security or who have a great deal. Why weren't they calling you before you had money?

❏ See page 62 for tips about stock distributions or fund pay-out decisions from 401(k), pension, employee stock plans and other tax deferred company savings or retirement benefit plans.

Be aware that you may pay large taxes and penalties on this type of tax-deferred money if it's not "rolled over" into another tax-deferred investment within 60 days of payout.

❏ See chapters 5, 6 and 7 for further information on how to match your money related goals with the appropriate investment strategies and products.

❏ Before you invest, learn about the risks, fees, returns and other features of the investment options you're considering. Since the financial community was deregulated in 1980, the investment options and alternatives are becoming endless and can be quite confusing. There are more and more ways to make money and lose it, too!

❏ Don't be a sucker. Don't let hucksters and con artists lead you by the nose. Become informed. Use caution. Be wise!

Future: Worries About Death and Survivors

Are worried about what your family would do, if you or your spouse were to die suddenly.

❒ Regularly review the adequacy of your insurance. Consider your age, the retirement assets you've accumulated and the financial needs of your spouse and dependents.

❒ Be sure to have an official and good quality:

○ Will in place.
○ Living-Will in place (read on for tips regarding both of these wills).

❒ Review each of the above wills at least once a year and update as needed.

❒ Be sure to discuss and have on paper where important documents and contacts are, such as: stock certificates, bonds, will, account books, insurance agents, brokers, living trust papers, special letters or videotapes to family members, maintenance schedules of home and cars and funeral arrangements.

❒ Consider the benefits of a living trust to avoid the attorneys and corresponding fees that can erode your life savings.

❒ If you have a lot of anxiety about death, you can do a number of things, such as: contact a pastor or rabbi; study the scriptures and other literature of your faith; read other literature about life and death; discuss these subjects with wise others; and contact your Employee Assistance Program (EAP) for assistance and referral to other appropriate professionals.

Wills

Are thinking about putting together a will.

❒ Resist wanting to delay having a good quality will. Having no will or a simple, but incomplete will NOW, can cost a lot in attorney fees and can take a lot of time. If you haven't made appropriate provisions in your will for what happens to the estate after the surviving spouse dies, then much or all of the estate may have to go through probate before the children or other beneficiaries receive a penny.

❒ Before going to an attorney, write down your answers to these questions:

Wills (continued)

○ Who do you want to get what from your estate?

○ Who* do you want to be the executor of your estate?

○ Who* do you want to be the custodian of your dependent children?

○ Who* do you want to get what and be executor of your estate when the surviving spouse dies?

* Be sure to discuss these responsibilities with these people and make sure that they agree to them, before you decide. Don't just drop the surprise of a heavy responsibility on somebody.

Living Wills

You are thinking about putting together a living will.

❏ Many people exhaust their retirement savings on medical expenses within the last two years of life. In many of these situations, the individual may be in an irreversible vegetative condition for weeks, months or years before dying.

Some of these situations would not have occured if "heroic" medical care had not been attempted in an effort to keep the body alive--at all costs-- regardless of the ability to recover and the person's quality of life.

❏ Sadly, the medical expenses (that were futile anyway) may leave little or no money for the spouse to survive on. This situation and any oustanding debts will only add to the emotional burdens and stress on the survivors.

❏ A good living will allows you to specifiy in advance when you want and do not want "herioc" medical care.

❏ Resist not wanting to have a living will. Our fears of death and "it can't happen to me" or "it's not my time" attitudes can be financially disastrous to those we love.

Debts Worry

You are worried about your debts and money and don't think you can pay off all your debts.

❏ Pages 69 through 81 will show if there is any possible way you can pay off your debts.

Late Payments
and Ignoring
Calls and Notices

You are late or not paying bills, and ignoring calls and letters from creditors or have just received a nasty note from a credit collection agency.

❏ Resist avoiding the calls and notices. Ignoring them is the worst thing you can do. It suggests to the creditors that you are irresponsible and that legal action against you such as wage or property liens, repossession, foreclosure and litigation may be the only solution to get what's owed.

❏ Work through the payment plan and tips in chapter 5.

❏ Call your creditors and explain when and how they will get their money. Do what you say you will do. Broken promises will be handled harshly. If you don't handle this stage of your problem properly, your blood pressure and levels of stress may become higher than you ever dreamed.

❏ Remember, phone calls and small regular payments are a small price to pay to keep from losing your house, car, or affecting your credit record.

Foreclosure

You have just received a notice of foreclosure.

❏ They can't evict you the next day, but do not treat this lightly.

❏ The only reason it's gotten this far is because you have consistently ignored them or not done what you said you would do.

❏ Depending upon the state you live in, the process of forclosure may allow you six or more months to work out your debt problem. After that, if you still have not worked it out, foreclosure (the loss of your home) is inevitable.

❏ Foreclosure will tarnish your credit record significantly (seven or more years) because the ability to manage a home mortgage is one of the key indicators used by financial lenders to assess financial responsibility.

❏ There may also be serious tax consequences. This depends upon how much your property is eventually sold for, and the amount of your mortgage balance. Any mortgage debt forgiven in excess of the amount received by the lender from a foreclosure sale is considered taxable income that you must pay taxes on.

❏ If selling your property is the only way out, then get on with it.

Bankruptcy

You are considering bankruptcy.

Whether a financial problem was caused by a family situation, illness, or simple lack of discipline, many people feel the helplessness, anger and even the disbelief of being in financial trouble. They often reach a point where they feel there is no alternative except to file for bankruptcy.

To help people cope with this situation, Congress has modified the original bankruptcy laws that were instituted in the 1930s with the Bankruptcy Reform Act of 1978. In addition to the Federal government, bankruptcy laws are also regulated by every state. Each can have its own rules regarding wage garnishment and distribution of the assets of a bankrupt person.

In some situations, you can voluntarily file for bankruptcy on your own. In other cases, your creditors can involuntarily force you into bankruptcy. In either case, the guilt, anxiety, confusion and frustration of bankruptcy should make this your last resort to getting out of financial trouble.

This section will explain the two major types of bankruptcy. It will also indicate the steps to take, the consequences and the cautions you need to be aware of if you decide to go this route.

Before deciding to file bankruptcy, you should make a firm determination to honestly assess how you got into trouble in the first place. You will then need to take the appropriate steps and have the perseverance to live within your financial means in the future.

This section is intended to be an overview only. You will more than likely need additional information from an attorney regarding the specifics of the state in which you live.

Chapter 13 Bankruptcy

Filing for Chapter 13 bankruptcy allows an individual two primary benefits.

❑ Creditors have to stop harassing you with either phone calls or letters.

❑ A payment plan over a period of time, usually over two to four-years, is worked out with all creditors.

This procedure usually allows an individual to keep all of his/her property while the payment plan is being made.

However, there are certain eligibility requirements that have to be met before an individual can file under Chapter 13, such as:

❏ The individual must be able to show that he/she has a job and a means of sticking to the payment plan.

❏ The individual must list all assets, debts and a breakdown of income and expenses in detail. The court then reviews this information and the proposed payment plan to make sure it is reasonable.

A Less Complicated Option

Before considering Chapter 13:

❏ Work through the payment plan indicated in the following chapter to determine how much you can pay on a monthly basis to each creditor.

❏ Then, call each creditor and indicate that you have made a personal commitment to instill the discipline in your spending habits necessary to pay off your debts. Indicate how much you will pay on a regular basis which should give them the time frame for when they will get their money.

Remember, the above two steps are basically the same procedure as Chapter 13 bankruptcy, but it does not stain your credit record.

The Chapter 13 just discussed is designed to work out a payment plan over a period of time so your creditors get all or most of their money.

Chapter 7 Bankruptcy

Chapter 7, however, is the liquidation of nearly all your debts through the sale of your property.

This method is usually reserved as a last resort and is for individuals who no longer have an income. If a person is unemployed, doesn't have much property and is simply overwhelmed by the amount of the debts, with no prospects of paying them off, then Chapter 7 is one option to eliminate the problem.

As with all of these issues, there are advantages and disadvantages. A primary advantage of Chapter 7 is that the law allows you to keep a certain portion of some assets. As an example, depending upon your state law, you can keep certain items such as the tools of your trade that allow you to earn a living. Also, most states let you keep a certain amount of your household furnishings and clothing. Others also let you keep a certain amount of equity in your personal residence up to a dollar amount of say $5,000. The main thing to remember is that you will not be completely destitute.

A primary disadvantage of Chapter 7 is that some debts cannot be cancelled. This means that even after you have liquidated your assets and paid off other creditors, you still owe these debts. Examples include debts to a current or former spouse, and alimony payments.

This also includes certain taxes, debts to government agencies other than taxes, and student education loans. Once again, this is only a sample of the types of debts you cannot wipe out. You will have to review your list of debts with an attorney if you decide to take this route.

Another disadvantage of this chapter is that you cannot file for this type of bankruptcy again for six years. Under Chapter 13, you do not have this same waiting period.

Remember the main difference between Chapters 7 and 13 is that Chapter 7 is a complete liquidation of most of your debts. Chapter 13 is an extended payment plan.

❏ If you are unemployed and simply must go Chapter 7, that should be an easier decision.

❏ However, if you are employed, you should work through the payment plan explained in chapter 5. This will show how possible it is and how long it will take to repay your debts.

Bankruptcies and Your Credit Record

❏ Bankruptcy is a last resort for financial problems so before taking that step, make sure you have looked at all avenues of repaying your debts. Bankruptcy can stay on your credit record for up to ten years depending upon the credit bureau in your area. This can make it more difficult for you to obtain credit later which can drastically affect your future lifestyle.

Be Wise About Lawyers

❏ If you have done these steps and really need to file bankruptcy, find a lawyer who specializes in this area to help you with the paper work. It is an extremely complicated and confusing set of rules, regulations and paperwork where one mistake can cost you a lot of money. Some attorneys now advertise their specialties in the yellow pages, but you should be cautious when looking at your alternatives. Some attorneys would encourage you to file bankruptcy simply to generate some additional revenues for themselves.

Credit Agencies and
Credit Counselors

In some major metropolitan areas, there are CONSUMER CREDIT COUNSELORS or AGENCIES that help individuals work out a payment plan. These counselors act on your behalf to discuss a potential payment plan with a creditor. They either charge a set fee or a small percentage of your income to work through your debt situation.

Some agencies are actually sponsored by creditors. This is a way for them to help people work through their problems. This way the creditors eventually get their money back. They can be found in the "Credit and Debt Counseling" section of the yellow pages.

Loan Consolidations

Be on the lookout for debt consolidation services. These organizations are listed in the same section. However, they essentially want you to consolidate your small debts into one large debt to them.

The problem is, they usually charge extremely high interest rates (up to 38%!) and stretch out your payments over a long period of time.

The idea is to look at these alternatives, but make sure you understand which type of service the organization is providing and what it will cost you.

❑   Be very cautious about organizations that simply want to consolidate your smaller bills into one large payment. In some cases, where you are in the final payments of a two or three-year loan, it is not to your advantage to consolidate the payment. This is described in more detail in chapter 6, Commercial Cautions.

Lawsuits

You are being sued.

It's difficult to offer suggestions in this area because there are different types of lawsuits--injury, property, business, personal, compensatory, friendly, nuisance, infringement, hostile, etc. Here are a few very general thoughts to consider:

❑   Don't panic. Keep a clear head.

❑   Begin collecting the facts about the case. You will need to have these when you talk to an attorney or in a few instances when you may elect to represent yourself.

❑   Resist talking directly to others about the lawsuit-- especially the party that is suing you and his/her attorney.

❑   Contact the right attorney for the kind of lawsuit you have. The field of law is like the field of medicine. There are many different specialists out there. For example, you may need an attorney who specializes in personal injury lawsuits, or one that specializes in real estate law.

❑   Some lawyers and law firms will allow you a free consultation, which is your opportunity to discuss the lawsuit, clarify what kind it is and ask if they have ever handled lawsuits like this. If they say yes, then ask how the cases turned out. Ask for references and follow-up on the references.

❑   You may be able to find attorneys through the yellow pages of the phone book, the state bar association and recommendations from friends and contacts.

❑   Prose (pro-say) courts may be an option depending upon the type of suit and where you live. Prose courts are courts for small claims where you can represent yourself--kind of like People's Court. You'll need to contact an attorney, district attorney or court system to determine whether a Prose court exists in your area and/or whether this is an option for your lawsuit.

❑   Think twice about representing yourself. Carefully consider the pros and cons.

❑   If you do elect to represent yourself, do your homework.   Study books that may offer tips.

Basic Needs

Food

Can barely afford food for you or your family.

❑ Check churches in your local area. Many of them have food pantries and other outreach resources for families in crisis. The American Red Cross and Salvation Army are also options. All of these groups may also be able to refer you to other community services.

❑ Buy and prepare high-value foods (those that have great nutritional value) for very little money. These include foods from the starch and bread family such as breads, noodles and other pasta, rice, potatos, corn, flours (for breads, pancakes, waffles, muffins, etc.) and other foods. Any kind of peas or beans have a lot of protein and fiber for a very low cost. Eggs, milk and yogurt are great low-cost sources of protein and other key nutrients. Buy fresh and frozen vegetables, and any meats on sale. *Eating these kinds of foods is not only a budget saver, but also very healthy because they are high in fiber and protein and low in fat, calories and salt.*

❑ Read and apply the other food tips in chapter 5.

❑ Ask friends and family members if they can help you out in these tight times.

Housing

Are about to be evicted and have no place to stay.

❑ Check churches in your local area. Some of them may have outreach programs for individuals and families in crisis. They may also be able to refer you to church-based temporary shelters or to other community agencies.

❑ Check with the county health department, department of housing, Salvation Army, American Red Cross, United Way and other community mental health services. Some of them may have outreach programs, resources and referral services that may be of support.

Medical

You need basic or emergency medical care but don't think you can afford it.

❑ Contact the county health department and United Way for special services and clinics where people with little or no income can get medical care.

❑ Most hospitals are required by either a sense of mission or the law to provide emergency stabilizing care to the needy.

❑ Refer to the medical section in chapter 5 for more ideas.

Major Medical
Expense(s)

You have just experienced a major unexpected unaffordable expense, or are about to have medical services that may be fairly costly (this may include having a child or family member with a major sickness or disability).

❐ Read your medical/health plan literature. Make the phone calls required before receiving certain services. Try to use doctors, hospitals and other providers that are in the plan network. Be sure to call when calls are required — when in doubt, CALL! Remember, for most medical plans (insurance, PPO and HMO), the financial penalties can become quite steep if you do not use the plan according to the rules and requirements.

❐ Ask your doctor key questions in advance, such as how unnecessary risks and costs can be avoided — e.g., using generic drugs, outpatient services, etc..

❐ Refer to the medical section in chapter 5 for more ideas.

❐ Watch for errors on bills and absurd overcharging. Bring these to the attention of the insurance company and the party involved. You can often get help from your insurance company or the benefits department of your company for best handling these situations.

❐ Contact the physician, clinic or hospital you owe money to just like you would any other creditor. If things are tight right now, advise them of a payment plan that is realistic for you and them.

❐ In some cases for the very poor, the bill may be forgiven. Don't count on this though as hospitals are experiencing worse and worse financial times.

❐ For major medical expenses of a sensational and/or tragic nature (quintuplets, major accident with many family members injured, rare expensive illness, etc.) have friends contact reporters at local newspapers and news stations (radio and TV). The news has often been instrumental in supporting and spreading the word about the situation and offering information about special fundraising efforts to support the individuals or family.

❐ Note: Shriner's Hospitals, Ronald McDonald Houses, United Way, county health departments and other groups offer various individuals with certain conditions and situations access to special medical programs, funds or services at little to no expense to you. *Be sure to check these out!*

Rent Goes Up

You just found out your rent increased a lot for next year.

❑ Move to a less expensive place.

❑ Consider getting one or more roommates to share expenses.

❑ See chapter 5 for more tips.

Accident

You just got into an accident or were in some type of disaster (tornado, earthquake) and home, cars or other things were damaged. Assuming all emergency medical, food and shelter needs are taken care of:

❑ Get any official reports NOW that may be needed to verify the incident such as: police reports on an auto accident or robbery, insurance agent or assessment reports on property damage to home or possessions.

❑ Write down all information regarding the incident and damages NOW--while your memory is fresh.

❑ Document the damages using a camera or video recorder.

❑ Review all applicable insurance policies: homeowners, renters, auto, liability, repair, warranties, medical, life, accidental death and disability.

❑ Retrieve any applicable documents that verify the existence and value of the items damaged, including photographs, videos, receipts and official appraisals.

❑ Contact the insurance agents of applicable policies for clarifications, procedures and help to file claims.

❑ File claims carefully and promptly.

❑ Be accurate as it may be difficult or impossible to file again to compensate for original claims that under estimated the damages. Accuracy would also help you to wisely avoid filing fraudulent claims.

Feeling Depressed ...
Even Suicidal

You are feeling very anxious, depressed--perhaps even suicidal about your financial problems.

❏ If desperately suicidal, call 411, operator or see the yellow pages for the number of a suicide crisis line. Or, call a good friend or Employee Assistance Program for temporary support.

❏ Read chapter 6 and complete exercise 6.1. Regularly review and fine-tune your list from this exercise.

❏ Learn to forgive yourself. Everyone is human and makes mistakes. However, it is important to learn from your mistakes and history so that mistakes are avoided in the future. Chapter 2 can help you to avoid problems in the future.

❏ If you haven't already, get a clear picture of what your financial situation really is. Sometimes problems seem bigger than they actually are. Read and complete chapter 3 to help you get a clear picture of where you are now.

❏ Remember, money is important but it isn't everything.

❏ Seek financial encouragement and practical support from a credit counseling agency. Remember, these people have probably helped a lot of others work out debt problems in situations like yours.

If you have growing worries or concerns about your situation (debts, use of alcohol and other drugs, gambling, past and other things) or your view of yourself, guilt, and other related feelings, you can do a number of constructive things, such as:

- Read good books and articles regarding your situation and concerns (eg: gambling, addictions, compuslions, low self-esteem, relationship problems, etc.);
- Study the scriptures and other literature of your faith regarding your situation, thoughts and feelings;
- Discuss these concerns with wise family members, friends and others in your life ... for guidance and encouragement;
- Contact a qualified pastoral counselor at a local faith community; and
- If available through your employer, contact the Employee Assistance Program (EAP) for assistance and referral to other appropriate professionals.

Alcohol and Drugs

You are considering drinking or doing drugs to make yourself feel better or forget about your financial and other problems or simply are thinking about experimenting with drugs.

❏ Remind yourself that these substances will:

   ○ Distort your ability to think with a clear head and your ability to make wise decisions.

   ○ Make you feel better about the circumstances, but any improved feelings WILL be temporary. The old feelings WILL return when the alcohol or drug levels decrease--and you WILL feel like you need more alcohol or drugs to feel better again.

   ○ Begin to suck your money right out of your pockets. It WILL be just like throwing it out the window. You will have nothing to show for it--and have everything to risk for it.

❏ Read chapters 2 and 6 for additional insights and tips on building a better stronger you.

❏ Remember, money is important but it isn't everything.

❏ Remember, alcohol and illegal drugs may be tempting but they are NOT irresistible.

❏ To improve your resistance, read chapters 2 and 6. Complete exercise 6.1. Regularly review, reflect and fine-tune your list.

❏ Finally, remind yourself that experimenting with illegal drugs is like playing Russian roulette. One shot can ruin your life or put you a step closer down the pathway of a lot of needless pain, losses and suffering.

Gambling

You are gambling or playing the lotto to try to earn income or solve your financial problems.

❒   Read chapters 2 and 6 for additional insights and tips for building a better stronger you.   Complete exercise 6.1. Regularly review and fine-tune your list.

❒   If you haven't already, get a clear picture of what your financial situation really is. Sometimes problems seem bigger than they actually are. Read and complete chapter 3 to help you get a clear picture of where you are now.

❒   Remember, money is important but it isn't everything. And gambling may be tempting, but it's not irresistible.

❒   See the box on page 58 for some additional ideas.

Spouse

You are having difficulty discussing and agreeing about money matters with your spouse.

❒   Read chapters 2 and 6. Complete exercise 6.1. Regularly review and fine-tune your list.

❒   If you are concerned or wonder a lot about your marriage and how you communicate about money and other matters, you can do a number of things, such as:

○   read and discuss this workbook with your spouse.

○   attend a financial education program together.

○   contact any available Employee Assistance Program for assistance and referral to appropriate support groups and professionals (if needed).

High Pressure
Brokers and Agents

**You are being called by a fast-talking,
high-pressure broker or insurance agent.**

❑   Resist being overwhelmed by brokers or agents
who are charismatic, fast-talking and those who
want you to rush into a decision or who try to make
you feel guilty for not investing:

❑   Here are a few things you can tell them:

○   You already work with a broker or agent you
trust and are satisfied with.

○   You invest independently, do your own
homework and use a discount broker.

○   You have no money to invest or risk at this
time.

○   You don't appreciate being called at work or
home at this time.   Your time with family and
at work is an investment you do not wish to
compromise

Investments, Economy and
Insurance

Stock Dropping

**You just found out some stock you have is
dropping lower and lower.**

❑   Remember, you will lose money only if you sell it
lower than you bought it.

❑   Consider whether this investment is for short, mid-
or long-term goals. Consider the historical
performance of the company, what you read and
feel about the company, its management, its future
and the market in general. Consider the losses of
selling it now, and the potential gains of holding on
to it if you can afford to.

❑   If it seems wise and you can, hang on to it and be
patient. If you bought it as an investment-savings
vehicle for mid- to long-term financial goals, it may
very well recover and be even better by the time
you need to convert this asset to cash or some
other investment.

❑   If you need to sell it, do so and take your losses
and don't look behind. Playing the market is like
gambling and sports. You win and lose sometimes.
Roll with the punches as best you can.   Learn all
about the experience so you can be smarter on the
next investment and not repeat the same mistakes
in the future.

ESOP

Many now have the option of diversifying funds in an ESOP (Employee Stock Ownership) plan.

Diversifications

Many ESOP plans begin offering employees who reach age 55 the option to diversify some of their ESOP stock.

"Diversify" simply means taking an amount of ESOP stock, selling it and then reinvesting the proceeds into another tax-deferred investment vehicle like a fixed fund or a diversified mutual fund--whatever options may be available.

Here are a few things to consider regarding diversification:

❐   Compare the stock price and potential for growth against "safety" of interest earnings (e.g. 401(k) Fixed Fund)

❐   Use caution when considering a diversification to an equity-type mutual fund as this may result in a possible loss of principal.

❐   Remember, you lose the "floor price" on the shares you diversify ... FOREVER.

❐   Also, in most ESOP plans you can't re-transfer diversified funds back into the ESOP plan.

Lump Sum Distribution

You just received (or are about to receive) a fairly large sum of stock or cash from an ESOP plan--also known as an ESOP Lump Sum Distribution or a 401(k).

❐   If you are still working, every attempt should be made to roll-over the full amount (or as large amount) as possible into a tax-deferred investment vehicle. This will allow you to defer (and ultimately spread) the tax liability and, in most cases, avoid the 10% penalty generally applicable to amounts distributed before the age of 55.

❐   If you may need access to the money (to make ends meet) consider rolling the full amount over into a "safe and liquid" type IRA account (e.g. savings account, money market mutual fund, etc.) and withdraw only the amounts needed as a last resort.

❐   Resist the temptation to spend this money on big-dollar perishable items --- things that will be decreasing in value over time, such as: new car, boat, or fur coat.

❐   If necessary, consider using this money as a down payment for a home, but keep in mind the steep tax bite if not rolled over into a tax deferred vehicle.

❐   Remember, if not rolled over, the distribution amount will be added to that years taxable earnings, possibly putting you in a higher tax bracket.

Insurance

Are wondering if your insurance is adequate or are overlooking some things insurance-wise.

❐ Be sure to regularly re-assess the adequacy of your various types of insurance. Here are some key times to do this:

<u>Home-Owners or Apartment Insurance</u>
❐ When your home (real estate) has significantly appreciated or depreciated;
❐ When you've made improvements in your home.
❐ When you've made major purchases of furniture, computer, tools, home office equipment, etc.
❐ When you receive large gifts or inheritances of major financial value (jewelry, furniture, etc.)

<u>Auto</u>
❐ When you buy or receive a new or used car.
❐ When your new car becomes 3-5 years old.
❐ If you ever rent cars (see next page).

<u>Life Insurance</u>
❐ When you've paid off your mortgage and other major debts.
❐ When all the kids are on their own.
❐ When you have met your retirement asset goals (usually an amount that equals or exceeds your total amount of life insurance).
❐ When other major life events affect you or your family.

<u>Mortgage Insurance</u>
❐ When you can find a term life insurance policy of equal or greater value for a better price.

<u>Medical</u>
❐ When you need to add a family member for coverage (spouse, new or adopted child, etc.).
❐ When you need to drop a family member's coverage (child over 21 or out of college, spouse or older child get's own less expensive coverage through another employer, death, etc.).

Note: *Before making changes, be sure to think through any tax, legal, insurance and investment implications. Consider getting wise counsel from your financial management adisory board (see pages 2 and 123).*

continued ...

Insurance (continued)

❑ For rental cars, think twice before you initial for the extra collision insurance. You may already be covered under your own auto insurance policy.

❑ At least once a year, re-read your auto policies. This also applies to your other insurance policies.

❑ Call your insurance agent for rate adjustments:

    ○ When your high school drivers go to college.

    ○ As your car(s) get older.

❑ Before buying, increasing or changing any insurance, do your homework.

    ○ Read related Consumer Reports articles.

    ○ Shop around for the best prices for the coverage needed — with your current agent, others and credible Internet sites.

    ○ Tell the agents you are shopping around for good coverage, service and prices.

    ○ If you are consolidating, changing or replacing policies, don't cancel any of the old ones, until the new policy is in effect.

❑ *You should maintain updated documentation of all the things you own and their value. This can be done by a combination of written records and receipts, photos or video recordings. Keep a copy of your documentation in a fire-proof file, safe or place outside the home (safe deposit box or at work).*

Chapter 5

Immediate Actions

A. *Take Advantage of Goal-Driven Budgeting*

Again, the real power of budgeting comes in as you increase your awareness of what you spend and begin to make planned changes to achieve certain goals.

The following tips and tools should help you to get a handle on your budgeting so that it becomes more goal-driven.

If you have never worked with a budget, we offer you an easy budgeting process to begin using. If you have worked with budgeting before, you still may want to read the next few pages as a review and to see if there are any new insights that can help you to fine-tune your budgeting.

Make Copies

Briefly review the budget format on page 69 Notice that each page represents two months. Make as many copies of this budget worksheet as you need for the next year or two.

Next, notice that there are two columns for each month. One column is for what you estimate, or budget, for that particular expense. The other is the actual amount of the expense.

Estimate

First you will need to budget, or estimate, your expenses for the next 12 months.   If you did exercise 3.5 (page 41), you can carry over the information from that worksheet. If you haven't done that exercise, go back and do it.

Don't forget to project expenses not paid on a regular monthly basis. Projecting for the next 12 months will help you plan for those expenses. You should now fill in the budgeted figures for the next 12 months on the blank budget forms. This should take about two to three hours to complete.

Simple Records System

The simplest recordkeeping system possible for keeping track of your expenses is to pay as many expenses as possible through your checkbook. This system will easily allow you to fill in the actual amounts spent each month. Then, have an envelope marked "Expenses Paid by Check." Put all receipts for check expenses in this envelope.   If you pay for something with cash, get a receipt and at the end of the day put those receipts in another envelope marked "Expenses Paid by Cash." Try to keep cash expenses at a minimum because spending cash is where many people lose sight of where all the money goes.

| At the End of Each Month | At the end of each month, simply sit down with your checkbook and your envelope for "Expenses Paid By Cash." Take each amount from your checkbook and put it on the proper line on the budget format. |

Group the receipts in your envelope marked "Expenses Paid by Cash" in the five or more categories on which you might spend cash. These might include food, gasoline, entertainment, etc.

Then list the cash expenses from your receipts on the proper line. Notice on the budget format the "c/cb/cc" in the actual expense columns (page 69). "C" means the expense was paid with cash and "cb" means it was paid through your checkbook. For expenses paid in cash, place a "c" next to that figure. Place a "cb" next to expenses paid by check, and a "cc" for expenses paid by credit card.

This is an extremely easy budgeting format to follow. It will allow you to see where and how you are spending your money. And, this easy budgeting process should give you some ideas about where to save extra money for other more important goals that you may have.

Notice that with this budgeting system, credit card purchases are not considered for each line of expense.

Credit Cards and Budgets

Using credit cards can really complicate the budgeting process. First of all, credit card purchases for this month are not paid for until at least the next month. When less than the full amount is paid, credit card purchases may not actually be paid off until months down the road.

This is how credit cards can distort your budget and make it more difficult to find ways of better managing your money.

Small Investment with Big Returns

So, with the easy budgeting process we recommend, you put the total of what you pay the credit card companies each month on the line under loan payments. This helps you to keep a clear picture of the cash going in and out of your budget. It keeps separate what you might owe from prior expenses which should be recorded on your list of liabilities — money owed to others.

You would be amazed at how little time it takes to fill in your actual expenses on a monthly basis. If you write out 30 checks a month, it will not take more than one minute to put each check amount on the proper line. It will also not take more than 15 minutes to group your cash receipts into the major categories.

With this approach, <u>it should take you less than one hour each month</u> to make sure you are sticking to your budget and saving for your goals.

If you stop to think about it, most of us work 40 hours per week or 160 hours per month to generate our income. Isn't it well worth the one hour a month it takes to find out where that money is going?

The following is a recap of suggestions for the actual preparation of the budget:

- ❏ Husband and wife must both participate in the budgeting process. If both spouses do not follow the budget, it simply will not work.
- ❏ Project income and expenses for the next 12 months.
- ❏ Insert the actual monthly expenses once a month.
- ❏ Compare your actual to the budgeted figures.
- ❏ Modify your spending habits if necessary.
- ❏ Alter your budget if major changes take place in your personal life, such as marriage, divorce or death.
- ❏ Encourage your children to perform basic budgeting practices.

If this budget seems like something that would be good for you, make a note on your "TO-DO" list to complete this on a monthly basis.

Exercise 5.1: Budget Worksheet

Month = _____   Month = _____

		Budgeted	Actual (C/CB/CC)	Budgeted	Actual (C/CB/CC)
Income	Net Salary	$_____	$_____	$_____	$_____
	Other Incomes	$_____	$_____	$_____	$_____
A. TOTAL INCOME		$_____	$_____	$_____	$_____

Expense Areas (some lines from exercise 3.5 (page 41) are combined)

		Budgeted	Actual	Budgeted	Actual
Residence	Mortgage/Rent, Taxes	$_____	$_____	$_____	$_____
	Repairs, Maintenance, Improvements	$_____	$_____	$_____	$_____
Utilities	Gas and Electric	$_____	$_____	$_____	$_____
	Phone: Home, Mobile, Pager & Other	$_____	$_____	$_____	$_____
	City: Sewer, Water & Garbage	$_____	$_____	$_____	$_____
Insurance	Life and Disability	$_____	$_____	$_____	$_____
	Health: Medical, Dental, Rx, Vision	$_____	$_____	$_____	$_____
	Auto	$_____	$_____	$_____	$_____
	Homeowners & Property	$_____	$_____	$_____	$_____
Loan Payments	Auto Loan(s)	$_____	$_____	$_____	$_____
	Credit Card(s)	$_____	$_____	$_____	$_____
	Student Loan(s) & Other Loans	$_____	$_____	$_____	$_____
	Equity Loan(s)	$_____	$_____	$_____	$_____
Food	Groceries	$_____	$_____	$_____	$_____
	Eating Out, Treats, Coffee, Soda, etc.	$_____	$_____	$_____	$_____
Clothing: work, social, play and sports		$_____	$_____	$_____	$_____
Health: all other reimbursed and non-reimbursed bills		$_____	$_____	$_____	$_____
Retirement Savings (not listed in exercise 3.4)		$_____	$_____	$_____	$_____
Non-Retirement Savings (not listed in exercise 3.4)		$_____	$_____	$_____	$_____
Business Related Expenses: including those reimbursed		$_____	$_____	$_____	$_____
Travel	Auto, Gas, Maintenance, Repairs	$_____	$_____	$_____	$_____
	Fares: Train, Bus, Air, Cab, etc.	$_____	$_____	$_____	$_____
Education	Newspapers, Publications, Books, Tapes	$_____	$_____	$_____	$_____
	Tuition, Fees, Computer (HW/SW), Internet	$_____	$_____	$_____	$_____
Contributions	Churches, Synagogues, Other Faith Groups	$_____	$_____	$_____	$_____
	Charities, Scouts & Other Causes	$_____	$_____	$_____	$_____
Recreation	Holidays, Vacations, Camps & Get-Aways	$_____	$_____	$_____	$_____
	Pool, Y, Health Club, Golf & Other Fees	$_____	$_____	$_____	$_____
	Museums, Zoos & Other Cultural Activities	$_____	$_____	$_____	$_____
	Events (sports, concerts, movies)	$_____	$_____	$_____	$_____
	Videos, CDs, Tapes & Electronic Games	$_____	$_____	$_____	$_____
	Photos & Hobbies (equipment & supplies)	$_____	$_____	$_____	$_____
	Cable or Satellite TV	$_____	$_____	$_____	$_____
	Other Equip. & Fees (sports, camping)	$_____	$_____	$_____	$_____
Miscellaneous	Child Care, Allowances	$_____	$_____	$_____	$_____
	Hair & Cosmetics	$_____	$_____	$_____	$_____
	Legal, Accounting & Other Prof'l Fees	$_____	$_____	$_____	$_____
	Appliances, Furniture & Tools	$_____	$_____	$_____	$_____
	Child Support &/or Alimony	$_____	$_____	$_____	$_____
	Gifts, Games & Toys (not listed above)	$_____	$_____	$_____	$_____
	Alcohol, Tobacco, Drugs &/or Bars	$_____	$_____	$_____	$_____
	Lottos, Racetracks & Other Gambling	$_____	$_____	$_____	$_____
	Tickets, Fines & Bail	$_____	$_____	$_____	$_____
	Cash Unknown & Other	$_____	$_____	$_____	$_____
B. TOTAL EXPENSES		$_____	$_____	$_____	$_____
C. NET SPENDABLE/GOAL INCOME (A-B) =		$_____	$_____	$_____	$_____

B. Cutting Expenses and Squeezing Out Some Extra Dollars

Review the following checklists to cut your expenses. First, indicate the things you are currently doing to manage your money. Then, indicate in the second column the one you will strive to do starting today, or specify when you'll start in the near future.

Review these lists often. The more you review them, the more likely they will become a way of thinking.

		I already do this.	I will do this starting: Now or Date
General Practices	Purchase items at sale/mark-down times of the year, and watch for post-seasonal and post-holiday sales on food, clothing, home supplies and other goods.	Yes	Now _____
	Watch newspapers and catalogs for sales and prices on all necessary items.	Yes	Now _____
	Try to buy house or generic label brands.	Yes	Now _____
	Shop selectively by noticing when an item is sold cheaper at one store than at another.	Yes	Now _____
	Use discount coupons.	Yes	Now _____
	Buy nonperishable canned and necessity items in bulk quantities on sale.	Yes	Now _____
	Shop with a list and buy only what is on the list.	Yes	Now _____
	Shop without the children, if possible.	Yes	Now _____
	Try to buy only what you need.	Yes	Now _____
	Avoid impulse buying.	Yes	Now _____
	Consider quality and service as well as price.	Yes	Now _____
	Shop at discount stores, off-price outlet stores, or factory outlet stores.	Yes	Now _____
	Before you buy, do your homework and review relevant articles in *Consumer Reports* and other reviews.	Yes	Now _____

		I already do this.	I will do this starting: Now or Date
Health	Drive safely, wear seat belts and never drive under the influence of alcohol or drugs (any amount).	Yes	Now _____
	Buy generic whenever possible. Insist on it with your doctor regarding prescription drugs.	Yes	Now _____
	Get and use one or more good books on personal and family medical care. These can help you have a better idea of how to handle many common health problems and when to see a doctor.	Yes	Now _____
	See if you can tough out your sniffles or aches without buying some over-the-counter drugs to make you feel better. Be sure to use your books on personal and family medical care to make informed decisions.	Yes	Now _____
	Jump through the hoops of your medical plan. Call and comply when it's required. This should help you to avoid unnecessary health care as well as needless expenses.	Yes	Now _____
	Take care of yourself. Eliminate destructive thoughts, habits and lifestyles. Eat and sleep well. Stay active. Make time for rest and quiet reflection. Strive to enjoy people and life. Monitor yourself for early warning signs of problems; then move quickly and wisely to treat them and minimize their severity.	Yes	Now _____
Insurance and Warranties	When shopping for insurance, try to get a range of insurance coverage quotes from different companies.	Yes	Now _____
	Shop for quality, coverage and service, as well as price.	Yes	Now _____
	Consider adjusting deductibles upward after the car is two to three years old.	Yes	Now _____
	Regarding auto and other rentals, think twice about special premiums that waive deductibles.	Yes	Now _____
	Think carefully about extended warranties and service agreements, especially on appliances. Is the quality of the product that bad that you need to buy service insurance on it? Look for products with good warranties that require no extra money.	Yes	Now _____
	See page 63 for other considerations. Be sure to discuss these matters with your insurance agent(s).	Yes	Now _____

		I already do this.	I will do this starting: Now or Date
Home and Utilities	If single, consider getting one or more roommates to share the costs of rent and utilities.	Yes	Now _____
	In winter, turn the heat down when not at home, and just before you go to bed. In summer, turn the AC down when not home. Do it manually or invest in a programmable thermostat.	Yes	Now _____
	In summer, use AC as a last resort after open windows and fans have failed to cool you off.	Yes	Now _____
	Keep lights off when not in use or needed for security.	Yes	Now _____
	Use the energy-saver cycles on dish washers, dryers and washing machines.	Yes	Now _____
	Use lower wattage bulbs wherever you can.	Yes	Now _____
	Call long-distance at lower rate times during evenings, weekends and holidays.	Yes	Now _____
	Alternate who initiates call with other party.	Yes	Now _____
	Avoid the use of 1-900 telephone services. Make sure the kids know your rule and punishment!	Yes	Now _____
	If your annual income is increasing, think twice about getting a newer and better place to live. People tend to buy bigger homes and let their spending lifestyle rise as income goes up. Resist this temptation. If you've been living fairly well on prior lower income, stash away the future raises and bonuses into savings and investments for the things you really need, retirement or causes you believe in.	Yes	Now _____
Food	Compare prices on a unit basis (per ounce or pound) and shop with a calculator to help figure this out.	Yes	Now _____
	Make healthy casseroles, stews, chunky soups and turkeys that last for several meals.	Yes	Now _____
	Plan meals around sales.	Yes	Now _____
	Shop once a week.	Yes	Now _____
	Try not to shop when hungry.	Yes	Now _____
	Plant a garden.	Yes	Now _____

	I already do this.	I will do this starting: Now or Date
Take advantage of food co-ops.	Yes	Now _____
Avoid frequent buying at convenience stores.	Yes	Now _____
Make your meals and bring them to work.	Yes	Now _____
Travel smart with coolers, homemade sandwiches and other food, drinks and snacks from the grocery store.	Yes	Now _____
Keep junk foods, drinks and treats high in fat, salt and sugar down to 20% or less of your total food budget.	Yes	Now _____
For family and friend food gatherings, go pot-luck.	Yes	Now _____

Recreation and Entertainment

Take less expensive vacations. Go camping or visit with friends more often, instead of staying at hotels and resorts. Be careful not to wear out the welcome mat and be sure to let friends stay with you, so they can save money, too.	Yes	Now _____
If it's more cost-effective, consider getting the annual membership instead of paying more expensive non-member admission fees (at museums, zoos, pools, Ys, and health clubs).	Yes	Now _____
If NOT needed at this time, drop fee-based memberships from organizations. Stand strong when you get the pleading renewal letters and calls.	Yes	Now _____
Reduce the number of events and activities you attend that involve costly admission fees and expenses for food and drinks, such as sports, concerts and movies. For example: Do you really need to be in that bowling league? Think of all the fees, beer and food you spend money on. Do you have to go so often or drink and eat so much?	Yes	Now _____
Consult your local public library before you buy CDs, tapes, albums, or videos. Many libraries have excellent selections that can be checked out either free or for a very small fee.	Yes	Now _____
Stop buying so many videos, CDs, tapes and electronic-computer games. Having the "latest" as soon as it's out can turn into a costly obsession! If you must see it or hear it, consider borrowing a friends or renting.	Yes	Now _____

		I already do this.	I will do this starting: Now or Date
Recreation and Entertainment (Continued)	Get out of the "monthly" clubs (e.g.: CD, book, tape, toy or gun-of-the-month clubs)!	Yes	Now _____
	Reduce the number of cable TV options you have or drop it all together. Depending upon the options chosen, cable TV can cost some families close to $400-$500 a year or more! Have you subscribed to Cable TV and found that you do not use it or that it consumes too much of your precious time?	Yes	Now _____
	Put expensive hobbies and interests on hold for now, or cut down on them, such as: downhill skiing, expensive restaurants and wines, hockey, tennis, golfing or horseback riding. Consider less expensive alternatives such as bicycle riding, gourmet meals at home, cross-country skiing, or the local Y.	Yes	Now _____
Travel	Car pool when you can to work, church, outings with the kids, family events and other places.	Yes	Now _____
	Walk or bicycle when you can.	Yes	Now _____
	Look for less expensive parking.	Yes	Now _____
	Maintain your vehicles and touch up paint chips and rust spots right away.	Yes	Now _____
	Use public transportation when you can.	Yes	Now _____
	Get the best air fares by watching for ads in the paper and making reservations weeks or months in advance.	Yes	Now _____
	Shop around for the best hotel rates. Remember, it's usually only a place to stay for less than 15 hours.	Yes	Now _____
	See the Food section (page 72) for travel food tips.	Yes	Now _____
	Repair your auto or bike instead of getting a new one.	Yes	Now _____
	Consider living without a car, especially if you live in a big city with good public transportation. Sell it or store it. Think of what you could save on payments, insurance, gas, parking and tickets. And think of how much exercise you'll get and how much less stressful life could be!	Yes	Now _____

		I already do this.	I will do this starting: Now or Date

Education

Drop subscriptions to papers and magazines you are not reading. Take advantage of the publications in your local public library. After all, you are already helping to pay for them through your taxes! — Yes — Now _____

Buy used books instead of new ones. You can always use a different color pen for your notations. — Yes — Now _____

Before you buy books or educational tapes, consult your local public library, or lending library at work. — Yes — Now _____

Try to offset tuition and fees through scholarships and employer-sponsored tuition reimbursement benefits. — Yes — Now _____

Miscellaneous

Find a cheaper place to get your hair, nails or face done. Aren't there cheaper places you can get them done just as well? Or are you paying for prestige? Is the price difference worth the sacrifice regarding your financial goals? — Yes — Now _____

Consider making gifts and cards (for birthdays and holidays) instead of buying them. — Yes — Now _____

Repair appliances instead of replacing them. — Yes — Now _____

Do what you can to cut down on money you spend on traffic tickets, court costs, fines, penalties and bail. Don't speed, drive recklessly or under the influence. Don't get in fights. Stay away from gangs, drug dealers, gamblers, fast talking sales people, brokers and other shady characters who promise you fortunes the easy way. Pay your taxes. Live an honest life. — Yes — Now _____

When going out with friends who have kids, too, consider getting the kids together at one house with one or two sitters. Depending upon the number of kids, you can pay the sitters well and still save money. — Yes — Now _____

Cut down on the amount of money you spend on alcohol at home or in bars and lounges. — Yes — Now _____

		I already do this.	I will do this starting: Now or Date

Miscellaneous (continued)

Never start using illegal drugs.   Yes   Now _____

Get help and stop if you are.   Yes   Now _____

Drugs can drain the money right out of your pockets and every paycheck.   These habits can quickly cost $50 or more a day.

Most users start lying, cheating, stealing, gambling and doing business in less than honest ways just to support their habit.   Stay away from them.

Never start using tobacco in any form. Stop or cut down if you do. You will begin saving money immediately on tobacco and dry cleaning. Don't forget about the thousands of dollars you'll save in the future by avoiding emphysema, heart attacks and cancers.   Yes   Now _____

Cut down on how much you are spending on the lotto or on other forms of gambling--yes, even bingo! Play the long shot without using your money. Participate in sweepstakes that don't require you to buy anything.   Yes   Now _____

If you can't afford to lose the money, don't play the stock market. Put it into something less risky like a savings bond, CD or money market.   Yes   Now _____

C. **Other Ways to Generate EXTRA MONEY**	You may want to use one or more of the following techniques to save or earn more money. List the ones on your "TO-DO" sheet which you can do.	*I already do this.*	*I will do this starting: Now or Date*
	Ask your current employer how you can do a better job and grow in responsibility and salary.	Yes	Now _____
	Look into a part-time job as long as your employer does not object.	Yes	Now _____
	Review every line on exercise 5.1 (page 69) and see if there are any other expenses you can cut.	Yes	Now _____
	Review every line in that exercise with your roommate(s) or spouse. Two or more people can often come up with many more ideas than just one person. In addition, you can help encourage and motivate each other to stick by the goals and agreements to cut expenses.	Yes	Now _____
	Consider having your children who have a regular full- or part-time job contribute part of their income toward rent, utilities, food and clothes. This is especially true for those out of high school or college and still living at home. You can always place what they are contributing into a forced savings account that they don't know about. Then, when they are ready to leave, get married or get a home, you can surprise them with a substantial amount of cash.	Yes	Now _____

D. WORKING OUT A PAYMENT PLAN

For those in debt trouble (large or small), it's also time to work out a payment plan. This will involve working with your information in chapter 3 and filling in the Proposed Payment Plan work sheet in this section; then you will have to make some phone calls to your creditors (the people you owe money to).

In the meantime, apply as many of the strategies you can from sections A, B and C from this chapter. This will help you to reduce spending and free up extra dollars to pay off your debts and begin saving some money.

You will also need to have a good debt payment plan that will satisfy your creditors, that won't break you, and that enables you to begin saving money for future needs and goals. The next two pages describe how to develop a payment plan.

First, review the completed work sheet below entitled <u>Sample Payment Plan</u>. Notice line A is simply the balance you owe to your creditors right now.

Line 1 may only be appropriate for some people. This payment is simply an amount of cash you may have on hand, cash you may borrow from a friend or relative, or cash from selling a particular asset. By making an initial payment to creditors, you will show good faith in wanting to pay them off. This will make it easier to work with them.

Next, notice that lines 2 through 21 show the total monthly payments and how much goes to each creditor. Keep in mind that the amount of your extra cash can change over a period of time. This can cause you to increase or decrease the amount of your payments.

Also, the initial amount of your debts and your extra cash will determine how many months you will need to eliminate your debts. One person may need 12 months, while another may need 18. Some debts may be paid off before others. This can increase the monthly payment on one debt that may have a high interest rate.

Now you should list your debts on the blank work sheet. Show the largest balance in the first column and then the next smallest, and so on. If you need more columns because you have a lot of debts, simply tape an additional sheet of paper to the blank payment page. You can continue listing your creditors on the additional sheet.

<u>SAMPLE PAYMENT PLAN</u>: Example that Results in Paying Off Debts Over aTwo-Year Period.

C R E D I T O R S   N A M E

	DATE	DESCRIPTION	TOTAL		VISA		MASTER CARD		DEPT STORE		GAS CARD		GAS CARD
A.	5-03	Beginning Balance	$6,000	=	$2,000	+	$1,500	+	$1,000	+	$1,000		$500
1.	5-03	Initial payment	-1,000	=	-400	+	-250	+	-150	+	-150	+	-50
2.	6-03	Monthly payment	-250	=	-75	+	-50	+	-50	+	-50	+	-25
3.	7-03	Monthly payment	-250	=	-75	+	-50	+	-50	+	-50	+	-25
4.	8-03	Monthly payment	-250	=	-75	+	-50	+	-50	+	-50	+	-25
5.	9-03	Monthly payment	-250	=	-75	+	-50	+	-50	+	-50	+	-25
6.	10-03	Monthly payment	-250	=	-75	+	-50	+	-50	+	-50	+	-25
7.	11-03	Monthly payment	-250	=	-75	+	-50	+	-50	+	-50	+	-25
8.	12-03	Monthly payment	-250	=	-75	+	-50	+	-50	+	-50	+	-25
9.	1-04	Monthly payment	-250	=	-75	+	-50	+	-50	+	-50	+	-25
10.	2-04	Monthly payment	-250	=	-75	+	-50	+	-50	+	-50	+	-25
11.	3-04	Monthly payment	-250	=	-75	+	-50	+	-50	+	-50	+	-25
12.	4-04	Monthly payment	-250	=	-75	+	-50	+	-50	+	-50	+	-25
13.	5-04	Monthly payment	-250	=	-75	+	-50	+	-50	+	-50	+	-25
14.	6-04	Monthly payment	-250	=	-75	+	-50	+	-50	+	-50	+	-25
15.	7-04	Monthly payment	-250	=	-75	+	-50	+	-50	+	-50	+	-25
16.	8-04	Monthly payment	-250	=	-75	+	-50	+	-50	+	-50	+	-25
17.	9-04	Monthly payment	-250	=	-75	+	-50	+	-50	+	-50	+	-25
18.	10-04	Monthly payment	-250	=	-75	+	-50	+	-50	+	-50	+	-25
19.	11-04	Monthly payment	-250	=	-75	+	-150	+	--	+	---	+	-25
20.	12-04	Monthly payment	-250	=	-100	+	-150	+	--	+	---	+	--
21.	1-05	Monthly payment	-250	=	-150	+	-100	+	--	+	---	+	--
		Ending balance *	-0-		-0-		-0-		-0-		-0-		-0-

* NOTE: Interest expense accumulated may require some additional payments.

If you do have some cash, you can use it to make an initial payment, and record that payment on line one. If possible try to pay off smaller balances first so that you can have fewer creditors to deal with while feeling a sense of progress as you pay them off. You should also try to pay some of the money on your biggest debts.

Now go back to the budget worksheet on page 69. Get the figure which is the extra cash you have left after paying your expenses. This money can be used to reduce your debts. Spread this amount to your different creditors. Make sure you are at least paying the minimum amount due on each debt. Try spreading the extra cash with the largest amount going to the largest debt.

Then you should complete the work sheet month-by-month. This way you can see the point where you will have all the debts paid off. Make sure this is done in pencil because you may make a lot of changes. Then you can call your creditors, explain what you are doing, and give them an indication of when they will be paid off.

A critical thing to remember is that once you make this commitment to your creditors, <u>you</u> <u>must</u> <u>stick</u> <u>with</u> <u>it</u>. When a promise is made and then broken, creditors and landlords get very upset. That is when they tend to proceed with legal actions and continued harassment. This makes the situation more stressful. Remember to be realistic and have the determination and perseverance to stick with your plan.

EXERCISE 5.2 PROPOSED PAYMENT PLAN

For paying off debts over a period from _____ **to** _____

Tip: Use a copy of this form, or create a similar form on a computer spreadsheet (creating formulas to do the math).

CREDITORS NAME
(list all credit cards with unpaid balances/amounts due)

DATE	DESCRIPTION	TOTAL					
_____	Beginning Balance	$_____	= $_____	$_____	$_____	$_____	$_____
_____	Initial payment	-_____	= -_____	-_____	-_____	-_____	-_____
_____	Monthly payment	-_____	= -_____	-_____	-_____	-_____	-_____
_____	Monthly payment	-_____	= -_____	-_____	-_____	-_____	-_____
_____	Monthly payment	-_____	= -_____	-_____	-_____	-_____	-_____
_____	Monthly payment	-_____	= -_____	-_____	-_____	-_____	-_____
_____	Monthly payment	-_____	= -_____	-_____	-_____	-_____	-_____
_____	Monthly payment	-_____	= -_____	-_____	-_____	-_____	-_____
_____	Monthly payment	-_____	= -_____	-_____	-_____	-_____	-_____
_____	Monthly payment	-_____	= -_____	-_____	-_____	-_____	-_____
_____	Monthly payment	-_____	= -_____	-_____	-_____	-_____	-_____
_____	Monthly payment	-_____	= -_____	-_____	-_____	-_____	-_____
_____	Monthly payment	-_____	= -_____	-_____	-_____	-_____	-_____
_____	Monthly payment	-_____	= -_____	-_____	-_____	-_____	-_____
_____	Monthly payment	-_____	= -_____	-_____	-_____	-_____	-_____
_____	Monthly payment	-_____	= -_____	-_____	-_____	-_____	-_____
_____	Monthly payment	-_____	= -_____	-_____	-_____	-_____	-_____
_____	Monthly payment	-_____	= -_____	-_____	-_____	-_____	-_____
_____	Monthly payment	-_____	= -_____	-_____	-_____	-_____	-_____

E. CONSUMER CAUTIONS

In the previous chapter we NOTED the cautions you should be aware of related to bankruptcy. However, there is a situation related to refinancing your debts that you should also know about.

If you have a lot of small debts in addition to a car payment, it can be tempting to get a debt consolidation loan and simply make one payment. There are two things you should be aware of before doing this.

First, you should be very careful about the interest rate on the new loan. Many debt consolidation loans charge as high as 20 or 30 percent interest on these loans. This is an outrageous rate which can cost you hundreds or even thousands of extra dollars. You should check with many different sources for this type of loan. Some might be your bank, credit union, or the lender where you have your home mortgage. Home equity loans have become very popular. However, remember that the money has to be paid back. Otherwise, the lender can take your house away.

APR

When comparing interest rates from one lender to another you should ask for the Annual Percentage Rate (APR). There are many different ways of stating and figuring interest rates. However, asking for this term will allow you to compare apples-to-apples. You should look for the lowest interest rate possible when checking with different sources.

Rule of 78's

You should also be aware of the Rule of 78's. This applies to fixed monthly payment loans, such as a car loan. It is the calculation that figures the amount of each payment that goes toward reducing the amount you borrowed. The following example indicates how interest is calculated on the Rule of 78's.

There are two important things to be aware of in this example. First, the interest you pay in the first six months is the majority of the interest charged for the entire 12-month period of time ($241.89 of the total $331.00). The last six months of this loan you are paying mostly principal and very little interest.

EXAMPLE:

($5,000.00 loan at 12% for 12 months)
Monthly Payments: $444.25 x 12 = $5,331.00
Total Interest = $5,331.00 - 5,000.00 (from above) = $331.00
Monthly interest computed as follows:
Add: 12 + 11 + 10 + 9 + 8 + 7 + 6 + 5 + 4 + 3 + 2 + 1 = 78   (Thus the Rule of 78's)

	IINTEREST PORTION	PRINCIPLE PORTION
1st Month's Interest = 12/78 x $331.00 =	$ 50.92	$ 393.33
2nd Month's Interest = 11/78 x $331.00 =	46.68	397.57
3rd Month's Interest = 10/78 x $331.00 =	42.44	401.81
4th Month's Interest = 9/78 x $331.00 =	38.19	406.06
5th Month's Interest = 8/78 x $331.00 =	33.95	410.30
6th Month's Interest = 7/78 x $331.00 =	29.71	414.54
Amount paid first 6 months	$241.89	$2,423.61
(Note the cost to borrow for only 6 months)		
Interest paid last 6 months	89.11	
Total Interest Paid	$331.00	

Secondly, if you refinance in the early months of the loan, you would not have paid off much of the money you borrowed. However, you would have paid a lot of interest. Therefore, if you refinance, you would start paying interest on the money you borrowed all over again. A more drastic example would be to refinance a three-year loan six months after taking it out. In this situation, you have not paid back much principal and simply start paying interest all over again.

F. CALLING CREDITORS: WHY, WHEN and WHAT TO SAY

This is another reason to work on a payment plan for your current debts.

If you don't call the people you owe, they begin to assume some things. First, they might assume you're a little tight on cash, on vacation or forgot to pay. Then, they send you reminder notices. If you don't respond to these notices, they might even call you.

If you don't return the calls or respond to about the second or third notice, they will assume you don't care and that you do not intend to pay what you owe. At this point they will begin to take legal action to collect what you owe them.

This may result in a threatening letter from an attorney or collection agency, or various legal actions such as a lien against your house, foreclosure on your home and/or court ordered wage garnishments. With a wage garnishment, your employer is notified of your irresponsibility and then has to deduct an amount from your pay check to pay off your debts. Read chapter 4 to learn how each of these can affect your life, in some cases, for many years!

So, when should you call those you owe? You only need to call them if you are (or will be) behind on your total bill or regular minimum payment(s). If this is the case, the sooner you call, the better. Ideally, you should call after you have worked out a payment plan using section D in this chapter. However, you can also call before this, advising them that you are now working out a payment plan and will get back to them. If you tell them this, then get back to them.

When you talk to them, be honest. Simply explain your situation and that you intend to pay what you owe. Then, explain how much you will pay, when, and how often.

Most creditors are human beings, too, and understand that people have tough times and sometimes get in over their head. They usually get tough with people they feel are lying, have no intention of paying and/or who are irresponsible who don't fulfill promises, commitments and obligations.

It might not be this simple if you borrow money from rip-off credit agencies or loan sharks. They may be much less patient and kind, and motivate you to pay in other ways. Watch out for the double and triple interest penalties. Watch out for your own and your family's welfare. Watch out for the easy way to pay off your debt by doing something shady. You'll pay forever.

Notes

Chapter 6

Goals, Life and Money

Goals and plans are important in many areas of life — relationships, work, family, education, retirement and money, to name a few.

Certain family, education, retirement and other goals require money to help make them happen. As you add up all these goals, the amount of money that you may need to meet all your needs and dreams also goes up. These include regular needs and desires, as much as the periodic, big-expense items such as a house, repairs and special vacations.

Knowledge is Power

Knowing what your goals in general are can help you to be a better planner regarding your life and your money. If you don't know what you need and want, it's hard to predict how much you'll spend, save and have left for the big things in life including retirement.

People who don't know what they want or need can agonize over decisions. Or, they can throw money away because they spend (or invest) on a whim, spontaneously without really considering some critical things. These people may either hate to go shopping (because they can't decide) or love to go shopping (because anything's OK).

What Influences Goals?

So knowing what you need and want is important. But there are other things to consider as well. It helps to know what influences your goals. Here are a few things to consider:

Internal Factors *Discussed in this Chapter*	*External Factors* *Discussed in Chapter 2*
A. Common Sense	Advertising and Sales
B. Foresight	Interaction with Spouse
C. Vision	Money Management Skills
D. Values	Ways of Decision Making Motives, Insane Thinking
E. Beliefs	
F. Discipline	Friends and Other People (past, present and future)
G. Goal Determination Exercises	Resources Available

Goals, Dreams and Other Stuff

A. Common Sense

Some people definitely know what they want, but they want things they can't afford or shouldn't spend money on considering where they are in life. They may have the best stereo, clothes, tools, CD collection, or jewelry, but they can barely meet daily living expenses and may be deeply in debt.

Many of these people may have goals, but they are short term and usually have to do with possessions. These people can be both victims and perpetuators of uncontrolled materialism. See chapter 4 for more about this and what to do about it.

B. Foresight

Part of good goal setting and common sense includes foresight — the ability to look ahead, anticipate and plan for things in the future.

C. Vision

Vision has to do with the scope of your thinking. For example, some people seem to think only about possessions or home regarding financial goals. Others only think about income needs for daily living expenses.

Here is an expanded list of goal areas to think about regarding now and the future:

General Goal Areas	*1-3 yrs*	*4-10 yrs*	*≥11 years*
debts			
emergency funds			
where you live			
vehicles			
possessions			
education & skills			
recreation & entertainment			
retirement			
helping others			
future generations			

Later in this chapter there is a larger blank worksheet for you to use to jot down your goals. But, before you get to that point, there are a few other things to discuss.

D. Values

What you value can strongly influence your commitments, goals, common sense and foresight. For example, valuing "newness and innovation" can result in buying things as soon as they are available, usually when they are the most expensive.

Think back for a moment how affordable calculators, computers, VCRs, CDs and TVs are now, compared to when they first entered the marketplace years ago.

Many of us have learned to value patience the hard, expensive way.

The list of things you can value is endless:

beauty	good looks	newness
sex	wisdom	convenience
discipline	happiness	safety
health	pleasure	youth
good relationships	owning things	getting older
truth	freedom	children
what others think	power	faith
money	control	being prepared
love	nature	helping others
security	growth	justice
integrity	honesty	spontaneousness
fairness	self-control	conservation
length of life	quality of life	more ... and more
empires	family	
commitments	being responsible	

Value Problems

How we value many of the above influences our thoughts and actions regarding money. Some of the problems that can exist in the area of values are discussed below.

❐ **Some people don't know what they value**. They never took the time to sort out what they value and what the priorities of those values are.

The role models in their life may have had no values or poor ones. During their youth these people may have had teachers, parents, other adults and peers who avoided expressing values or remained neutral on the subject of values. Unfortunately for some, this philosophy appears to have mutated into a "keep your opinion to yourself (or you'll commit political, occupational or social suicide)" paranoia.

People who don't know what they value may be more vulnerable to advertising, fast-talking and peer pressure. These people set themselves up for being controlled by others. If they want to take greater control over their lives these people need to do some soul searching. It's going to take some studying, questioning and challenging of what's read. It requires an open mind, and a desire for the truth. It is tough to do, but not impossible.

❏ **Some people have an unhealthy emphasis on certain values.**
What happens to people who overvalue fashion, newness,
pleasing others, not making waves, good looks, money, what's in
vogue, possessions, pleasure or instant gratification?
Overvaluing these can add up to: disappointment, stress,
spending, emptiness, obsessions, compulsions, superficial
relationships, impatience and never being satisfied, many of which
influence thoughts and use of money.

❏ **Some people have distorted values.** They value being sneaky,
getting away with things or attaining money and power, at all
costs. They value themselves only. They don't care about others
or the environment. In fact, they may even take pleasure when
other people stumble and fall in life. Chapter 2 offers a few hopes
for these people.

E. Beliefs

Then there are your beliefs about yourself, others, money and
everything else in life. Your beliefs include all your outlooks,
assumptions, reasons, philosophies, predictions, guesses and
explanations. You use your beliefs to explain why you value
things.

What are your assumptions, and other beliefs about the following
things in life? *Discuss your beliefs about one or two of these
areas each day or week at meals with family and friends.*

Saving money	Giving ... Helping others
Loans ... Being in debt	Lending money
Being late	Credit cards
Dining out	Education of self and other family members
Drinking alcohol	Health
Commitments	Responsibilities
Absenteeism	Illegal drugs
Lying, cheating and stealing	Taking unfair advantage of others
Spending money	What "enough" or "having enough" is
Investments (bonds, stocks, cds, etc.)	The past and future
What others think of you	What life is all about
Gambling (even lotto, bingo)	Retirement
What you think of you (self-esteem)	Death
What you need ... What others need	What you think you deserve
What you want ... and what others want	Making sacrifices
How to get what you want and need	Security (job, pension, social security, etc.)

You've picked up your beliefs from your parents and other
role models in your life, your religion and faith, formal and
informal education, as well as your experiences and intuition.

Belief Problems

Some of this is pretty heavy stuff, but if you really think about it, your beliefs about these and other things also strongly influence the way you manage your money.   Like values, several problems can also exist regarding beliefs. Here are a few of the big ones:

❑ **Some people don't know what they believe or they forget what they believe.** This can be due to a lack of reading and education, not knowing the facts about life or specific things. It also can be due to a lack of good role models in life. Exposure to people who lie, cheat, steal and break promises can shape outlooks on life as well as abilities to share with and trust others. Finally, none of us is immune to forgetting what we believe. Our memories can fade.

We need to take the time to periodically review and fine-tune our beliefs and what we know to be true and worthy of our time, thoughts, energy and money.

❑ **Some have beliefs that are not true or could be overconfident.** In chapter 2, we already talked about the myths of credit cards, certain ads and sales pitches and other misconceptions about money.

Then there are people who deny reality. These people may not believe they will ever die, lose a job, get sick, get injured etc.   Others think they will never need to care for a sick or ailing spouse, child or parent. Others believe their pension and social security will be enough when they retire.

Others don't believe they have a problem with money, credit cards, relationships, alcohol or drugs. Others have unrealistic or distorted expectations about jobs, work, how to work with others, marriage, parenting, what others think, fashion, making money and spending money.

❑ **Some have distorted beliefs.** Whether rich or poor, some people are jerks. They believe it's OK to weasel out of bills and debts by playing games of delay, never being satisfied with the job, ambiguous words in contracts, etc.   These are the people who believe it's OK to fake an illness or injury, lie, cheat, steal or sue anybody to get money or revenge.

These are the people who think its OK to have no commitments to anyone but themselves. They think it's OK to make promises they can't keep, stab people in the back, or say things to please or manipulate people to get whatever they want.

F. Discipline

Discipline can mean different things to different people. As far as money management goes, discipline boils down to the ability to manage your life and money on a daily basis to attain your goals and meet current and future wants and needs. Discipline requires some of these strengths and abilities:

❏ Patience   ❏ Resistance to peer pressure

❏ Foresight   ❏ Resisting temptations to spend

❏ Encouragement   ❏ A good memory (remembering your values, beliefs and goals)

❏ Perseverance   ❏ Endurance

You may have noticed that much of what we've talked about is all interrelated. Values influence beliefs. Beliefs influence values. Beliefs and values are involved in your foresight, vision and discipline. All influence your goals, as well as your plans and abilities to achieve them.

Here are some general tips when setting goals and managing life to achieve them.

Get Smart and Stay Aware

Maintain Regular Awareness of Who You Are, Others and The World.

❏ Read chapter 2 regarding the forces influencing your thoughts and use of money.

❏ Read about and study the world you live in. Watch for forces that can influence you. Be wise.

❏ Focus on the best of the values and beliefs learned in your past. Screen out the less desirable ones.

❏ Study your religious beliefs and values. There may be much wisdom in what you read, hear and feel spiritually, regarding money, decisions and lifestyle. Your efforts may very well result in a wealth of prosperity for you and others.

❏ If married, understand the values and beliefs of your partner. Help your spouse to understand yours, too. Inspire one another to plan and manage together as a team regarding money and life.

❏ Regularly review your lists of key values and beliefs, reasons for living and related financial goals. Keep them fresh in your mind.

Get and Stay Real

Maintain Regular Reality Checks.

❏ Think periodically about inevitable events like retirement, aging and death. Do the same for likely events such as a job loss, severe sickness, untimely death or caring for an aging parent.

❏ Think through your options and plans regarding these inevitable and likely events NOW while you're calm and have a clear head.

❏ Remind yourself where you are in life regarding your skills, abilities, efforts, resources and opportunities. Be honest with yourself about areas you need to improve to advance and to meet your goals.

❏ Study and remind yourself of your weaknesses especially in the area of money management. These might include concerns about certain values and beliefs, discipline, bullheadedness, fantasies, flexibility, vision and foresight. *Don't forget to work on them!*

❏ Remind yourself of your obligations, commitments and responsibilities regarding you, others and your values and beliefs.

❏ Evaluate whether your goals and desires are wants or needs. Be honest about whether they are real needs.

❏ Study the risks, returns and other realities of your goals. Can you realistically achieve them? What are the potential tradeoffs and value, returns on investment? Be realistic.

❏ Are you sticking to your strategies and action plans to achieve your goals?

❏ Be honest with yourself and realistic about whether you should seek assistance for a specific problem or concern. Do you need to go to the library? See an accountant? Attorney? Church? Credit counseling service? Do you need to seek support through an employee assistance program?

❏ Avoid isolating yourself. Try not to avoid others who caringly challenge your thinking, ideas and lifestyle. Seek the company and counsel of those who encourage you to grow and improve in healthy ways.

Get and Stay Strong

Maintain Regular Discipline and Resistance.

☐ Discipline yourself not to deny or avoid reality.
Do not put off thinking about and constructively dealing with the realities of life, such as: problems, weaknesses, changes, challenges, family, work, life and death.

☐ Resist over-confidence and being a know-it-all.

☐ Resist basing all your choices and direction in life entirely on your feelings.

☐ Base most of your choices and direction in life on good solid beliefs, values and goals. Make these the main basis of where and how you travel through life and manage your money.

☐ Resist thinking that you deserve things and can get them the easy way.

☐ Resist out-of-control consumption and materialism.

☐ Resist self-centeredness and greed.

☐ Resist being easily fooled. Stand strong when in the presence of fast-talkers and con artists. Avoid them when you can.

☐ Resist lying to yourself and others about money and other matters in your life.

☐ Resist the temptation to cheat and be dishonest.

☐ Be resourceful and wise in where you get your insights, wisdom, strength, discipline and courage.

G. Goal Determination Exercises

It's time to move on to two critical exercises:

6.1   Exploring your values, goals and reasons for living. This is tough but not impossible!

6.2   Determining your money-related goals. This is best done after you explore your values, general beliefs and personal goals.

Examples of how to do these exercises are included with both 6.1 and 6.2.

Note: Both of these exercises may take some time to complete. Take your time and think these things through. Discuss them with the important people in your life.

Review and Up-Date Regularly

Review and update these exercises at least once a year. Some of your beliefs, values and goals may change as you move through life, being shaped by:

❐ Each new year, what you experience and learn, and the people in your life; and

❐ Key phases and events of life, such as: getting married, having children, seeing them grow, getting divorced, becoming a single parent, losing a job, retiring, death of a loved one, having a close encounter with death and others things.

If married, be sure each person completes each of the next two exercises. We suggest making a few copies of each worksheet and completing them individually. This will allow each of you plenty of time to jot down your thoughtful answers. When done, you can read and discuss each others answers and then merge them together on a separate copy.

Exploring Values, Goals, and Reasons For Living.

Below is an example of how to use the worksheet on the next page. The items listed are not necessarily ranked in order of importance. The important thing is to list all that come to mind. Note that this list should <u>NOT</u> include specific things that you would spend money on.

Example

When you do this exercise, also keep this in mind: Your list should be more of a general list of what makes you get up each day, the core of what makes you tick, the fabric of you, the way you think and live.

Important Values	Goals and Other Reasons for Living & Working
I Value .... I Treasure ...	*I Live for ... I Live to .....*

Character Traits
√ *peace*
√ *patience*
√ *wisdom*
√ *kindness*
√ *intelligence*
√ *self-control*
√ *love*
√ *strength*
√ *courage*
√ *doing best effort*
√ *working hard and smart*
√ *competency*
√ *being responsible*
√ *unselfishness*
√ *preparedness*
√ *quality work*
√ *honesty and trust*
√ *learning from mistakes*
√ *balance in life*
√ *proactive*

Relationships with:
√ *spouse*
√ *children*
√ *brothers, sisters, parents, etc.*
√ *good friends*
√ *co-workers, colleagues, customers ...*
√ *God*

other
√ *my faith*
√ *nature ... and being outdoors*
√ *financial independence*
√ *health (all areas)*
√ *quality of life*

Share and enjoy life with spouse, children, other family, friends--people in general.

Live and work in accordance with my faith, the character traits and other things I value.

Develop, apply and share my faith, skills, other abilities and resources, constructively, throughout life.

Help and encourage our children (and others) to prepare for, survive, grow and thrive in life.

Help others, environment and world improve through my work and other efforts.

Do the best I can in whatever I do without becoming an impaired perfectionist or workaholic.

Not deliberately let people down as long as it doesn't conflict with the key people and things I value.

See and appreciate other places, cultures and people around the world.

Prevent problems that can be prevented and minimize those that can be minimized.

Maintain financial independence until the day I die and leave a good amount for the future generations to build upon.

etc.

Exercise 6.1: Exploring YOUR values, goals and reasons for living.

Use this worksheet to list your over-all values, goals and reasons for living. Remember, this exercise requires some serious thinking and discussions with the important people in your life.   Resist the temptation to skip this exercise. Remember, how you answer this will shape and influence your money-related goals--now and later in life.

Important Values	Goals and Other Reasons for Living & Working
I Value ... I Treasure	*I Live for ... I Live to .....*

Determining Money Related Goals

One of the worst things you can do is to set goals and then not meet them. Or, worse yet, you could achieve "big" money-related or other goals .... then find out that they weren't nearly as important as other areas of your life that you neglected. Either situation would be frustrating or depressing. So, here are some words of wisdom to consider when setting your money-related goals:

❑ Be sure each goal matches up with the really important things and people in your life (your answers from the previous page).

❑ Avoid listing "pie-in-the-sky" goals and those that would require winning the lottery, a big inheritance, becoming a criminal or having an unlikely job.

❑ Be realistic. Be sure to list goals that, down deep, are goals you think you can achieve with some hard work and wise money management.

Now, think about your answers from the previous page and the areas below.
Use the next page to pencil-in your money-related short, mid and long-term goals.

EXAMPLE

General Money-Related Areas	Short-Term Goals within 1-3 years	Mid-Term Goals 4-10 years	Long-Term Goals 11 or more years
❑ Debts	• pay-off equity loan	• pay-off student/mortgage early	
❑ Emergency funds	• have $5000 in liquid assets for emergencies		
❑ Where you live	• major remodeling	• new AC, water heater, sump pump	• possible cabin at lake?
❑ Vehicles	• pay off car loans	• new car every 6-8 yrs/pay cash	
❑ Possessions	• new TV	• new stereo, some new furniture	
❑ Education	• pre-school for kids	• self and/or spouse to grad school? • musical instruments for kids?	• up to 3 kids in college or trade school at the same time
❑ Vacations, recreation and entertainment	• low-cost vacations • memberships	• kids at camp	• trips to Hawaii or Europe?
❑ Retirement	• save	• save	• no debts, able to meet needs, and enjoy life on 50% of current income
❑ Gifts, giving, helping others	• regularly give ≥10% to church, United Way, etc		• be able to help kids out with car for college
❑ Other		• possible adoption?	• kids wedding fund
Other Related Goal Areas			
❑ Job-career	• same job with at least cost of living increases	• major promotion/raise	• become teacher and consider possible decrease in pay
❑ Savings and investments	• save most of all raises, maximum savings in IRAs, manage investments wisely		
❑ Future generations	• develop and maintain will, living will and living trust		• plan gifts and estate to help kids out with first home, grandkids with college and/or special causes (church, medical, social, etc.)

PS: *Items from budget of regular living expenses should not be on this list.*

Exercise 6.2: Determining your money-related goals
List your money-related goals considering the categories below.

General Money-Related Areas	Short-Term Goals ... within 1-3 years	Mid-Term Goals ... 4-10 years	Long-Term Goals ... 11 or more years
❐ Debts			
❐ Emergency funds			
❐ Where you live			
❐ Vehicles, etc.			
❐ Possessions, etc.			
❐ Education			
❐ Vacations, recreation and entertainment			
❐ Retirement			
❐ Gifts, giving, helping others			
❐ Other			

Other Related Areas	Items from budget of regular living expenses should not be on this page.		
❐ Job-career			
❐ Savings and investments			
❐ Future generations			

Notes

Chapter 7

Making Your Goals Come True

The prior chapters should assist you to the point of:

❏ Being able to develop and operate on a goal-driven budgeting process.

❏ Having extra money to save and invest toward your goals.

❏ Doing some soul-searching about what's important in life and what some of your more important money related goals are.

What we haven't yet covered is determining how much your goals will cost and the specifics on how to achieve them. That's where this chapter comes in! Most of your money-related goals (from the last chapter) fall into three areas: income, spending and retirement goals. Common to these goals are a few others like career and pay, investments and earnings, and loans and debts.

Throughout this chapter, we will discuss each of these, but the focus will be on tips and tools to achieve money-related spending and retirement goals. Rather than just listing questions, tips and formulas, we organized everything into these steps:

Step 1

Project and Minimize the Costs of Your Goals
❏ Estimate the Costs of Your Goals
❏ Be Creative and Resourceful to Reduce the Costs

Step 2

Find and Commit the Dollars
❏ Stretch and Squeeze Your Spending
❏ Consider Extra Income

Step 3

***Make Your Money Work for You
versus You Working for Money***
❏ Learn the Powers, Look Into the Crystal Ball--
Then Do Some Math
❏ Match Goals with Best Investment Vehicles
❏ Don't Touch Your Goal Funds Until Ready

Step 4

Do It --Stay On Top of Things--and Celebrate
❏ Begin, Maintain and Update Your Action Plan
and Foundations
❏ Don't Forget About the Legal and Tax Issues
❏ Keep Learning, Stay Aware and Get Smarter
❏ Celebrate Successes

Let's take a look at each of these steps!

Next Steps .....

These tips and tools are based on years of personal experience and working with others to achieve their goals.   We do not offer any miracle solutions--just plain common sense, words of wisdom and a few tools.

What we share with you really does work. We've seen countless successes in many people's lives including our own.

So, grab some more coffee, tea, soda or water and hear us out for this last chapter. We've done our best to tell it like it is and how it can be!

OK, you've done your soul-searching and jotted down your goals, but how will you achieve them? It's time to examine and analyze your goals, the options and all the data.

This effort involves answering a number of questions and doing a little math. But, the true success will depend upon the quality and implementation of the plans you develop to achieve each goal. This is going to involve some logical thinking.

Some people don't like to be logical and analytical. They say it's not their nature or they're not very good at it. If this is you, ignore your bad feelings about logic. Certain times and challenges in life require some sound logic and thinking for the best solutions. Force yourself to think this chapter through and develop good plans. If you have a spouse who is more analytical, let him/her do the exercises. But work together and ask for coaching so you can learn along the way.

If you are fantastically rich, hire someone to coach you, administer your empire and keep you in line so you don't blow it all.

Step 1 Project and Minimize the Costs of Goals

Most of your goals from the last chapter either have to do with spending money in the future, or being sure that you have it in the future when you retire.

With each goal, you need to estimate what the total cost of that goal will be. To determine the costs, you need to answer some questions for spending goals and other questions for retirement goals. Let's see what the differences are.

In general, you will be able to achieve your spending goals either through savings and investments, or by financing them through loans. Which goals do you choose to or have to pay for in-full at the time of purchase? Which are you considering financing through a loan?

For each goal you think you'll finance, get the answers to these questions:

Exercise 7.1

Cost of Financed Goals.

Goal = _____

A. $_____ = Down Payment

B. _____ = Number of monthly payments

C. $_____ = Amount of monthly payment

D. $_____ = (B x C)

E. $_____ = All other fees and coverages associated with getting the loan (such as: points, appraisal, legal, insurance, title, application, credit checks, etc.)

F. $_____ = Total Cost of This Goal (A + D + E)

Exercise 7.2

**Cost of Goals
Paid in Full**

For the same goal on the previous page, determine the cost if you pay in full.   Get the answers to these questions:

A. $_____   =   Price of what you want to buy in the year of purchase

B. $_____   =   Applicable taxes and other fees

C. $_____   =   Total Cost of This Goal = A+B

It becomes obvious that financing becomes much more expensive. Financing adds up to additional costs. The way to keep your costs down is to pay in full at the time of purchase.

Realistically, this is not possible for most of us at various times in our life. We will probably need a loan to buy a house or car.

When getting a loan at these reasonable times, the challenge is to shop for the best rates to keep the interest and other costs of obtaining the loan as low as possible. Imagine the additional expenses that people incur who get loans on many things and who don't shop around for the best rates! For most of your goals, paying in full would save you a lot of money though you may have to save and wait to buy.

The Bottom Line

Regardless of what we say, it's a personal choice for each goal. It all boils down to: whether the additional costs of financing are going to be worth the ability to have the item early (with strings attached until you pay for it) *versus* waiting to buy it for less with no strings attached.

Much of this has to do with your patience, values, beliefs and other ways you think about money (chapter 2).

**Retirement
Planning**

Retirement goals are quite a bit different from spending goals. The key questions become:

- *How much income will you need?*
- *Will your expenses be more or less than before retiring?*
- *What kind of reserves will you need to live well throughout your retirement years?*
- *Considering your answers, how much should you be saving now to achieve your retirement goals?*

To determine this amount you should consider several factors. We could try to get very sophisticated and develop a complex formula that considers a person's age, inflation, the stock market trends, trends in health costs, etc. But this would involve much math and a lot of speculation.

Exercise 7.3

**Cost of
Retirement Goals**

A sophisticated estimate may be just as accurate as a simpler one using the formula below (and re-done regularly). When using this formula, it is important to redo your estimate about every one to two years to help you to adjust for changes in inflation, living expenses, social security and pension.

A. $_____ = Monthly Income Needed for Budget in Retirement Years. Use exercise 3.5 on page 41 to do a projected budget for your expenses in an average retirement year. Do your estimated retirement budget based on current living expenses and adjust for the following:

- SUBTRACT those expenses you expect not to have in retirement years, such as: mortgage, children's education, work-related commuting expenses, etc.; and

+ ADD those new expenses you probably will have at retirement, such as: monthly premiums for medical and dental insurance; emergency expenses (for possible major repair, medical); discretionary spending (for special traveling, gifts, major purchases and other money-related goals to achieve in retirement).

B. $_____ = Monthly Social Security benefit at Retirement.

C. $_____ = Monthly Pension payment(s) at retirement.

D. $_____ = Total Minimum Monthly Income Needed from Assets = (A - B - C)

E. $_____ = Total Minimum Annual Income Needed from Assets = (D x 12)

F. $_____ = Total "Hands-Off" Investment Amount Required to Generate Annual Income (from interest, dividends, annuity payments ...). Use chart 2 on page 112 to determine the total investments needed to earn the amount you entered in E.

You may be shocked at how conservative we are and how big your number is, but consider the trends (and questions) on the following page.

Why Be So Conservative
and Proactive
About Retirement Goals?

Here are some good reasons to plan carefully regarding money and your retirement:

❑ The average life expectancy continues to climb and there are more people living beyond the age of 100 than ever before. How old do you anticipate living to, pessimistically and on the bright-side?

❑ To survive our increasingly global and competitive economic times and other challenges (some listed on this page), more and more companies are:

○ Curtailing lifetime "full" coverage of health benefits in retirement and making future retirees share in the cost of coverage out of their own money; and

○ Phasing-out pension plans that have the plan benefits dependent upon long-term employment, little to no portability, and/or that offer plan participants few to no opportunities to manage personal plan assets.

❑ More companies are replacing pension plans with Retirement Savings and other retirement plans that make you the administrator of your retirement assets and income in retirement. Most of these assets may currently be in stock. How familiar are you with the risks, how to minimize them and how to manage these assets for the best returns?

❑ Health costs are still out of control at double-digit annual inflation rates. What will be your health costs when you retire including monthly premiums, deductibles and co-pays? What if you exhaust the limits of the plan(s) you have?

❑ Consider the following regarding social security:
1) Social Security may not always keep up with inflation;
2) Because of the aging U.S. population, fewer people are contributing to it while more are depending on it;
3) Government leaders will continually be tempted to use Social Security reserves to pay-off the growing national debt; and 4) The true quality of its administration and adequecy of funding and reserves into the future are unknown. Will it be around when we retire, and if so, how adequate will it be for how many of our retirement years?

❑ In many locations property taxes are skyrocketing and other taxes continue to climb. Will you be able to pay the ones that go up or will you have to sell your home and move?

If you're smart, you'll play it safe and plan ahead for a worst case scenario. That way, if you're wrong and things turn out better than expected, you'll have more money to achieve more goals in retirement. You'll be pleasantly surprised instead of depressed and desperate!

"Work like you'll live to 100, and live like you'll die tomorrow."

Ben Franklin

Related Questions
❐   Other key questions are: Where can all your retirement money come from? How much of that annual income will you have to generate yourself? Consider the best and worst case scenarios.

❐   Do you want to work in your retirement years? How can you minimize the risk of having to liquidate (sell and cash in) assets to meet regular living expenses in retirement? Will you have to work in your retirement years? Will you be able to work?

Take some time to figure out how you'll pay for each goal (finance or cash .... via savings and investments) the costs of each spending goal <u>and</u> the cost of your retirement goals.

Use the worksheet on page 115 in this chapter to record and total these costs and when you expect to achieve the goals.

Be Creative to Reduce The Costs Of Your Goals

Soon, we will examine where this money can come from and how you can achieve the goals. But first, you may want to see if there is any way to reduce the costs of the goals. Read the next few pages for some ideas.

Merge Goals

Some goals may seem very costly. Or, maybe the total cost of all your goals makes them seem unattainable. You might be able to easily reduce the cost of some or many of your goals by doing a little resourceful and creative thinking.

Look at exercise 6.2 on page 95 and see if there are several financial goals you can merge together. In other words, are there several goals that can be achieved through a single investment or expense? Are there ways you can reduce some of your expenses over time, by a single investment now? Here are a few examples:

- Summer cottage now--becomes retirement home or retirement asset
- Bicycles now help to squeeze travel dollars over the long haul
- Energy efficiency improvements now help to squeeze dollars over the long haul
- Tools, workshop and hobbies now become money maker in retirement
- Trailer-Camper now cuts costs of annual family vacations and retirement travels
- Expenses of various goals that become tax deductible (such as mortgage interest, charitable contributions, expenses of projects or travels when helping others, etc.). These expenses achieve one or more goals and become a tax deduction.

Timing and Cost-Cutting	Did you ever buy something costly (furniture, airline tickets, auto, etc.), only to discover: • A sale on it days, weeks or months later? • The price dropped quite a bit by the end of the year? • You just missed the sale price by a few days or weeks? Did you ever think you might be able to save money if: • Your timing was better? • You had thought and acted ahead a little? Are you sometimes amazed at how some people: • Find the greatest bargains? • Were really smart about how they planned out a trip or vacation and saved a lot of money?
Travel	Here are a few timing and cost-cutting ideas to think about regarding your travel-related goals. ❏ If your job requires you to travel, you might be able to time a vacation with your business trip. If you were traveling to a destination for work and wanted to vacation there a few days, it doesn't hurt to see if you can extend your stay for your vacation days. At the very least, your business-related transportation expenses would be covered by the company. Even if your spouse and/or children were going, at least you would have your costs covered. ❏ If feasible, you could further reduce family travel costs by driving instead of flying. Again, if your trip was work related, the driving costs would be a business expense and probably less expensive to the company. Anything you can do to keep your costs down and the company's costs down is a real winner. ❏ When making airline reservations, call well in advance of when you need the tickets--the earlier the better. When you do call, ask the travel agent or reservationist for the cheapest fares, if they are nonrefundable and if there are any other restrictions on the tickets.
Bargain Hunting Tips	Ask about bargains, deals, special discounts, extended sale prices or early access to prices regarding a future sale even if you don't see any signs or ads. In general, you have more bargaining power and the sales-people have more incentive to win you over and help you if: • If you appear to be ready to buy today at the right price. • You are buying several "big ticket" items at once (e.g., two or more pieces of furniture, replacing several windows or remodeling several areas of the house, etc.

- The bigger the total bill is (over $300).

- You will be paying for the item or service in full (versus on their payment plan).

Remember, it never hurts to ask when it comes to bargains.

Sales　　　　❐ Be smart about seasonal sales, post-seasonal sales, closeouts and liquidation sales.

- You can get Christmas tree lights at 1/2 to 1/4 the cost if you buy them after Christmas.

- Prices also vary a lot on clothing depending upon the time of the year. Buy summer clothing after summer, and winter jackets after winter.

- If you're buying for the kids, be sure to consider how much they will grow by the time they will use the item. You may need to buy a larger size now.

Do It Yourself　　❐ When it comes to home repairs and improvements, it often saves to do it yourself. One of the tradeoffs is the cost of the tools you will need. You can offset these by renting tools or borrowing them (from family or friends). If you borrow, encourage others to borrow yours when needed, and insist on repairing or replacing whatever breaks while in your possession.

Friends　　❐ Remember moving, building, repair and other projects
Helping Friends　　go much quicker when friends tackle them together. Many of your friends may have much talent and experience in areas you know little about.

- Remember to be a great host and have plenty of food and drinks;

- Don't forget to say thanks; and

- Be sure to return the favors ... or initiate the help when they need it!

❐ See chapters 4 and 5 for many other cost cutting tips.

❐ Finally, keep seeking money saving ideas through discussions with friends, public TV and books at the library, bookstores and hardware stores. You might be able to get the costs of your goals down by getting others to pay for a portion of the costs.

Resourceful Funding

Company sponsored benefits may be able to help you out quite a bit, especially in the areas of health costs, retirement and educational goals.

Company Benefits

❏ Employee Stock Ownership Plans (ESOP) are a way to obtain company stock on a tax deferred basis. With ESOP plans you are earning this stock according to a formula usually based on salary and other factors. 401(k) savings plans are a way for you to save money for retirement oftentimes with the company matching a portion of whatever you save. This matching amount is usually in the form of stock and is added to your account throughout the year.

❏ Company-sponsored tuition reimbursement programs are a great way to reduce the expenses of your formal education be it trade school or courses toward a college degree. Most programs require you to get a certain grade or better to get reimbursed for the expenses covered under the tuition program. Even if these programs just cover 25% of the costs, that's 25% less that you have to pay.

❏ Health related benefit or insurance plans become invaluable to cover various costs of medical care that can often add up to huge dollars! Again, whatever costs that these plans cover, is that much less you have to pay!

If you ever think you will use these benefits, read your benefits materials and follow the requirements carefully. Most plans require calls and other requirements to get the maximum coverage. If you don't play by the rules, you will have to use more of your own money to pay the bills.

❏ Check the employee perks out at your company, such as:

- Tickets to museums, plays, sports events, etc.
- Discounts on company products, services, and rental cars.
- Access to consumer purchasing discount clubs and groups.
- Company store(s).
- Lodging and other facilities or resources that employees and family members can use.
- Company organized vacations.
- Free samples of products.
- Special scholarship programs for the children of employees.

❑ Perks may be well advertised or virtually unknown! Read your benefits materials, company newsletters and bulletin boards. Check with coworkers in human resources, corporate relations and other departments of your company. You may discover one or more perks that help to reduce the cost of your budget or your bigger goals.

❑ Sharing the costs of a major purchase goal may also be a feasible option for some people. It may be a home or property in the mountains or at a lake. It could be a trailer camper or something else.

Cost Sharing

Cost sharing can be a source of much friction if one or the other party is irresponsible, becomes unfair, inflexible or unreasonable. Be sure that the family members or friends you share with are trustworthy people. Be sure you discuss key things in advance, write out what you agree upon and do whatever must be done legally (contracts, agreements, wills) for joint purchases like these. Follow through with your end of the bargain and responsiblities.

Other ways to reduce costs through creative funding include:

Frequent Flyer Deals

❑ You may get the transportation or lodging costs for one or more family members covered through free passes you accumulate with all of your other traveling. You may also be able to get good deals, including free tickets, when you give up your reserved seat to help the airline and another passenger out at a time of overbooking or flight delays.

Scholarships

❑ Scholarships are very helpful when your kids go to college. Be sure to encourage them to study hard and perform well in their areas of talent.

Explore and apply for all scholarships available through the high school, community, governmnet and colleges being considered using college counselors and Internet sites.

These aren't all of the tips, but they are some of the more important ways to reduce the costs of some of your goals through creative funding. Keep on the look out for other ideas and be creative.

Step 2: **Find and Commit the Dollars**

Stretch and Squeeze Your Spending

What fat can you squeeze out of your current spending (budget) for money you can set aside for your goals? See chapters 2 and 5 for ways to avoid wasting money and ways to find some for your goals.

Once you squeeze this money out, you need to put it somewhere safe. A safe place is where it will grow and where you won't touch it,where you will nearly forget about it so you won't spend it!

If you've had some debt problems, hopefully in a short period of time, you'll be on the right track in managing your finances. Then, it will be time to start thinking about your short, medium and long-term personal financial goals.

If you had to work through a payment plan, you know you can squeeze and stretch extra money out of your paycheck. Once your debts are paid off, the trick is to take the money you were using to pay-off your debts and start saving that money. If you didn't have to work through a payment plan, use the suggestions in chapter 5 to help you find extra money.

Consider Extra Income

There may be ways you or family members can earn additional money to accelerate achieving your goals. See chapter 5 for ways to do this.

Remember to resist spending whatever additional income you earn. When you get a bonus, raise or inheritance save it for your "money-wise" goals, instead of spending it.

Depending upon where you put your goal money and how you invest it, your money can also generate income. This is what the next steps are all about.

Use Automatic Deposit

If you haven't already, look into savings plans which can automatically be taken out of your paycheck through your employer. Many companies offer a direct deposit to a particular savings account or a credit union. In many cases, you may also be able to purchase U.S. Savings Bonds through your payroll department.

Automatic (electronic) deposit and savings programs are simple and can be started by making a phone call to the payroll people. If these choices are not available, then check with your local bank for other savings opportunities.

Direct (automatic) deposit is a painless way to save. Once the money is taken out of your paycheck, you will learn to live without it. Automatic deposit makes regular saving convenient. It helps to make up for our shortcomings of forgetting to save or being tempted to spend everything in our paychecks.

If it's the right time for automatic payroll deductions, make a note on your "TO-DO" list to call your payroll department. The earlier you start, the better.

Do not get into the habit of constantly dipping into this savings. Developing a forced savings and sticking to your plan is the most important aspect of meeting financial goals. There is an old saying that is extremely important to remember: "Pay yourself (your goal savings funds) first!"

You will soon discover how disciplined savings and compounding can help you meet your goals. The next steps will show you how much to save for each of your goals, and how to make your money work for you.

Step 3: Make Your Money Work for You

... versus you working for money

By now, you have an idea about the total cost of some, many or all of your goals and you may be feeling that things are hopeless. Don't despair!

Let's see what really needs to be done and can be done!

First you need to learn the powers of compounding and tax deferral. There is really nothing magical about them. These powers are the result of some simple math.

Power of Compounding

What makes these powers important to you is how they can make a huge financial goal seem attainable and how they can make small regular savings grow into huge funds.

Compounding is simply earning interest on your interest. There are many different ways institutions figure the interest on your savings. Some accounts give you the interest daily, while others do so weekly, quarterly, semi-annually or annually.

How to Compare

When shopping for interest rates on your savings, you should ask for the "annual percentage yield." This rate takes into consideration whatever compounding method the institution is using. This number allows you to compare apples to apples.

Chart Tips

The following are three key concepts to understand about compounding and how it can result in large sums of money over time:

1.   The long-term effects of earning interest on interest can make a drastic difference in your savings.
2.   Discipline is required to maintain a consistent savings program.
3.   You should try to earn the highest interest rate possible while still protecting the safety of your money.

The compounding chart below shows how much a $50.00 per month deposit will accumulate to at different interest rates for the number of years indicated. Using this chart and and the example below should help you to see the power of compounding and be tools for calculating your own numbers.

Compounding Chart 1

With monthly compounding, if $50 is deposited each month:

For this many years:

At this annual interest rate:	3 years	5 years	10 years	20 years	30 years	It will grow to this amount:
5%	1,937.65	3,400.30	7,764.10	20,551.70	41,612.95	
6	1,966.80	3,488.50	8,193.95	23,102.05	50,225.75	
7	1,996.50	3,579.65	8,654.25	26,046.05	60,988.55	
8	2,026.80	3,673.85	9,147.30	29,451.00	74,517.95	
9	2,057.65	3,771.20	9,675.70	33,394.35	91,537.15	
10	2,089.10	3,871.85	10,242.25	37,968.45	113,024.40	
11	2,121.15	3,975.90	10,849.90	43,281.90	140,226.00	
12	2,153.85	4,083.50	11,501.95	49,462.75	174,748.20	
13	2,187.15	4,194.70	12,201.85	56,662.10	218,663.50	

Here's an example, using this chart to determine the difference in savings WITH and WITHOUT compounding.

Assumptions and Applicable Formulas	*Amount Accumulated WITH Compounding*	*Amount Accumulated WITHOUT Compounding*
(a) From chart 1 assuming $50.00 per month is deposited for 20 years, earning 10% interest, compounded monthly and leaving the interest to accumulate, and not touching any of the funds =	$37,968.45	
(b) Now, use the same situation as described above, except spending the interest that is earned. $50.00 X 12 months = $600.00. $600.00 X 20 (years) =		$12,000.00

Compounding Can
Be Motivating!

The previous example should point out what a difference compounding can make on your savings. The difference between 0% percent interest (when you spend the interest) and 10% interest compounded monthly (when you leave it to accumulate for 20 years) makes a big dollar difference ($37,968.45 - $12,000.00 = $25,968.45). Also note that if you put in $50.00 a month for another ten years, that amount reaches $113,024.40; almost three times as much! By looking at the long-term effects of compounding, it is possible to find new reasons and renewed motivation to save.

Being a Better
Shopper (Investor)
Pays ... BIG!!!

Now, look at chart 1 again. Assume a $50.00 deposit over a thirty year period of time at a 5% interest rate. In thirty years, the amount saved is $41,612.95. Not bad. Imagine, however, if you shopped for the highest interest rate available, say 13%, and let the money build over the same time period. In this case, you would have $218,633.50 -- a big increase -- all because you shopped for a higher interest rate.

Remember: Monthly deposits can accumulate quickly!

Compounding
+ Tax Deferral

Now let's combine the compounding concept with the idea of tax deferral. Tax deferral is simply earning interest and paying the taxes on that interest at a later time. Our tax system is progressive, which means that the more you make, the higher percentage you give to Uncle Sam.

As an example, a married couple, which has a taxable income of $35,000.00 per year, would pay about one-third (or 30 cents of every dollar) of interest earned to Uncle Sam.

Let's go back to our Compounding Chart 1. Let's go through a situation where an individual can earn 12 percent interest and pay the taxes each year, or earn the 12 percent in a deferred (i.e., 401(k), IRA) vehicle where the taxes are paid when you take the money out.

If you earn 12 percent and don't pay the taxes, notice the amount you have over a 30 year period of time -- $174,748.20. However, if you had to give one-third of that 12 percent (or 4 percent) to Uncle Sam each year, you would end up with only 8 percent return on your money.

Notice, 8 percent over 30 years amounts to only $74,517.95. That is more than $100,000.00 in Uncle Sam's pocket instead of in yours!!

Compounding and tax deferral can give you the incentive to do the steps we suggest in this program.

You can use the following chart and formulas in two ways:

A. To determine how much to put away on a monthly basis to meet your goals (needed for your goals achievement plans on page 115); and

B. To determine how much a regular amount of monthly savings will grow to over time.

Chart Tips

Let's see how it works.

Compounding Chart 2	Number of Years to Reach Goal or Number of Years of Regular Monthly Savings					
Annual Interest Rate	*3 years*	*5 years*	*10 years*	*20 years*	*30 years*	
5 %	39.8	68.0	155.3	411.0	832.3	Factor to Obtain and Use In Formulas Below
6	39.3	69.8	163.9	462.0	1,004.5	
7	39.9	71.6	173.1	520.9	1,220.0	
8	40.5	73.5	182.9	589.0	1,490.4	
9	41.1	75.4	193.5	667.9	1,830.7	
10	41.8	77.4	204.8	759.4	2,260.5	
11	42.4	79.5	217.0	865.6	2,804.5	
12	43.1	81.7	230.0	989.3	3,495.0	
13	43.7	83.9	244.0	1,133.2	4,373.3	

A. To determine how much to put away on a monthly basis to meet your goal, follow these steps:

1. Determine the number of years (___) you want to achieve your goal in, and the interest rate (___%) you'll get on your savings.

2. Using these numbers, find the factor on the chart above.

3. Divide the total dollar amount ($____) needed for your goal, by the factor (from the chart) to tell you how much to put away each month now.

B. To determine how much a regular amount of monthly savings will grow to over time, follow these steps:

1. Determine the number of years (____) you will be able to save and what interest rate (___%) you will be able to obtain on whatever you save.

2. Using these numbers, find the factor on the chart above.

3. Multiply the amount you can save each month ($___) by the factor (from the chart) to tell you the amount you will have after depositing that amount each month for the number of years specified in #1 (above).

The examples below show how the chart and formulas above can be used to determine how much you would have to save each month to achieve a goal, and then how much you could accumulate over time with a certain regular monthly savings.

EXAMPLE A: Let's assume you want to accumulate $15,000.00 in ten years to fund a child's education. If you know that you can earn 10% on your deposits, simply divide the $15,000.00 by the appropriate factor (204.8) and that tells you how much you will have to contribute monthly ($73.23) to have $15,000.00 in ten years ($15,000.00 divided by 204.8 = $73.24).

EXAMPLE B: Let's assume you knew you could squeeze $60.00 per month out of your budget and deposit that amount for 5 years. If you could earn 7% interest compounded monthly, you would accumulate $4,295.58 ($60.00 X 71.6 = $4,296).
Can you see how compounding makes financial goals seem much easier to accomplish?

Let's take some time to review the use of the charts and formulas from the last few pages. We'll do it through two quizzes to test your money management skills in the area of using compounding to determine goal achievement plans.

Study the compounding charts labeled 1 and 2 in this section. Think of these charts as tools that can guide you towards specific short, medium, and long term financial goals. Use the charts to solve the problems below.

Skill Test 1

> Problem situation = assume a deposit of $50.00 per month compounded monthly. Imagine that you can deposit $50.00 for 10 years at a 10% interest rate.
>
> Which of the goals listed below will be in your reach at the end of this period? (see Compounding Chart 1)
>
> A. A European vacation costing $10,242.25
> B. An additional room on your house costing $15,000

Skill Test 2

> Problem situation = imagine that you want to accumulate $50,000.00 for retirement in 30 years. Assume that you can earn 11% interest on your monthly deposit.
>
> How much do you have to put away each month to reach your goal? (hint: use formula from Compounding Chart 2.)
>
> A. $35.66 a month
> B. $17.83 a month

Once you are ready to start saving for your goals, you can use these compounding charts and formulas to fill out your goal achievement worksheet on page 115. These will help you figure out how much to put away monthly to meet those goals.
If your goals are at the end of a time frame not indicated in the chart, you can either estimate or purchase a calculator that can make these computations for you.

The answers are: Skill Test 1 = A, Skill Test 2 = B.

Some people set up separate savings vehicles for each goal so that each year so that they can keep funds separate and see the progress toward accomplishing that goal.

Review and Up-Date

Remember, interest rates change, the costs of your goals can change up or down and your priorities can change. You should make a note on your "TO-DO" list to review your plans periodically.

After you've learned the powers of compounding, figure out how many years you have to achieve one of your goals.

Exercise Tips

Then, look into your crystal ball and estimate what kind of annual compound interest rate you'll earn on the money you save or invest. Use a conservative interest rate based on interest rates at this time. *Remember to review and update your estimates about every 2 years to adjust for changes in the cost of your goals and interest rates.*

Now, take these three numbers (amount to save, interest rate and years to do it) and use Compounding Chart 2 to determine how much you need to save each month for how many years to achieve your goal. Do this for each of your goals.

Again, notice that money saved or invested grows very quickly, and in large amounts according to the following factors:

- The higher the interest rates or dividends are that you can earn;
- If the interest or dividends earned are compounded (reinvested into the fund);
- The more often the earnings are compounded (daily, weekly, monthly, quarterly);
- The longer you leave it in; and
- The less you dip into it.

The bottom line is this: If you are a wise and disciplined saver and investor, your money will begin to work for you and generate a lot more money. This is additional money (besides any regular income) made simply being smart and disciplined with your money and time.

With these keys to success, you can accumulate huge amounts of money to help accomplish what seemed to be impossible or unaffordable goals.

EXAMPLE ... of next page.

Top Short-Term Goals • 1-3 Years	Target Date	Pay By: Loan Inv.	Ways to Decrease Costs	Total Goal Cost	Investment Vehicle(s)	Interest Rate	Monthly Amount
DIFFERENT CAR IN	3 yRS	L ①	Buy used	$ 5,000	SAVINGS	5 %	$ 129
Remodel BATHROOM IN	3 yRS	L ①	Do most of the work by self with family/friends	$ 2,000	& money market	6 %	$ 51
Top Mid-Term Goals • 4-10 Years							
NEW CARPETING IN	5 yRS	L ①	shop/wAIT for sAles	$ 3,000	mutual funds	8 %	$ 42
college for oldest IN	10 yRS Ⓛ	①	• Apply for scholarships • kIDS work summer jobs • gIFTS from GRANDpARENTS	$ 15,000	"	10 %	$ 74
Top Long-Term Goals • 11 or More Years							
college for youngest IN	20 yRS Ⓛ	①	• STATE schools	$ 25,000	mutual funds	10 %	$ 33
VACATION Home/CABIN IN	20 yRS	L ①	shop Around	$ 60,000	"	10 %	$ 79

Exercise 7.4: Goal Achievement Plans

Jot down your goals for each category from chapter 6.

Then record your answers to the other columns using the questions, formulas and charts from this chapter.

Each year review and if necessary adjust them. Read below for reasons why.

Top Short-Term Goals • 1-3 Years	Target Date	Pay By: Loan Inv.	Ways to Decrease Costs	Total Goal Cost	Investment Vehicle(s)	Interest Rate	Monthly Amount
_____	_____	L I	_____	$_____	_____	____%	$_____
_____	_____	L I	_____	$_____	_____	____%	$_____
_____	_____	L I	_____	$_____	_____	____%	$_____
_____	_____	L I	_____	$_____	_____	____%	$_____
_____	_____	L I	_____	$_____	_____	____%	$_____
_____	_____	L I	_____	$_____	_____	____%	$_____

Top Mid-Term Goals • 4-10 Years

_____	_____	L I	_____	$_____	_____	____%	$_____
_____	_____	L I	_____	$_____	_____	____%	$_____
_____	_____	L I	_____	$_____	_____	____%	$_____
_____	_____	L I	_____	$_____	_____	____%	$_____
_____	_____	L I	_____	$_____	_____	____%	$_____
_____	_____	L I	_____	$_____	_____	____%	$_____

Top Long-Term Goals • 11 or More Years

_____	_____	L I	_____	$_____	_____	____%	$_____
_____	_____	L I	_____	$_____	_____	____%	$_____
_____	_____	L I	_____	$_____	_____	____%	$_____
_____	_____	L I	_____	$_____	_____	____%	$_____
_____	_____	L I	_____	$_____	_____	____%	$_____
_____	_____	L I	_____	$_____	_____	____%	$_____

$\longrightarrow$

Review and Up-Date This Worksheet Every 1-2 Years $\longrightarrow$ **Here's Why**

Remember: Your income, budget, and goals can and usually do change throughout your life. What's important to you when you're young or single, will be different than when you're married, have children, or are nearing retirement.

Also, the cost of a goal can go up or down. It's not unusual for electronic appliances (VCRs, video recorders, computers, microwaves, etc.) to go down a few years after introduction. And, real estate can go up or down over a short time depending upon the local economy, inflation and other factors.

Finally, investment options may change and interest rates can go up or down. How you manage your investments considering these and other changes can speed up or delay achieving your goals.

Investment Options
& Risks

Making your money work for you sounds great, but there are some challenges to be considered by the wise money manager. Here are some of the key challenges:

❒ The many different investment options (income, growth, tax benefit and speculative) and vehicles (see chart at right);

❒ Each investment's returns (what kind, when and how much money it makes or loses);

❒ Each investment's risks (safety--how secure your original investment will be and the reliability of the predicted returns);

❒ How each investment (and any returns, losses and other changes) will affect our taxes;

❒ How liquid the investment is (how easily it can be sold and converted to cash); and

❒ The additional costs of the investment (broker fees, commissions, points, spread, etc.).

The Wise Money
Manager

In a nutshell, the wise money manager strives to diversify a range of investments with good returns, while minimizing the risks, tax consequences and additional costs of the investments.

In addition, the wise money manager matches the goals in mind (including the potential needs for liquid assets) with the investment objectives and vehicles available.

We will not go into depth on all of the investment options and all considerations. This chapter will offer you some basics-- the tip of the iceberg. But, they are the basics that can start you on the path to achieving your goals.

By the time you finish this chapter, you should have a fairly good knowledge that:

❒ Regular savings and investments with compounded earnings will make you money,

❒ Matching goals with investment objectives (and investments) is a wise thing to do,

❒ You can shop around for better investments and earnings to make your money work better, but you have to be wise in what you do or you could lose a lot or all of it!

❒ The wise money manager has and uses a wise advisory board. Select yours carefully!

The Main Options	Income Investments	Growth Investments	Tax Benefit Investments	Speculative Investments
<u>Right</u> ➤➤ These are the 4 main categories of investment objectives we have the option of putting our savings into. <u>Below</u> ↙ You can see that the different investment vehicles satisfy one or more of these objectives.	Income investments generate a cash flow. However, you must pay taxes on that cash flow.	Growth investments increase in value; however, you do not pay taxes on that increase until you sell that investment.	**Tax Exempt Investments** • With these investments, you never have to pay taxes on the earnings. **Tax Deferral Investments** • Deferral simply means earning interest and not paying taxes on the interest until a later time. Some of these investments may have tax and other penalties when terms of the investment are broken (when you sell it prematurely, or don't roll it over within a specified time period).	These are also known as high risk or aggressive investments. These may have the potential for the highest yield but with very little safety, at the risk of you earning nothing and losing all of your investment. Be careful about these unless you can afford the higher risks of losing your money.

Some Investment Vehicles

Vehicle	Income Investments	Growth Investments	Tax Benefit Investments	Speculative Investments
Stocks	x	x		x
Bonds				
Corporate	x			
Government	x		x	
Municipal			x	
Government Securities				
Treasury Notes and Bonds	x			
Treasury Bills	x			
Government Agency Securities				
Reserves for S & Ls	x			
Reserves for Coop. (farmers)	x			
Mutual Funds				
Stocks	x	x		x
Money Markets	x			
Muncipal Bonds			x	
Government Paper	x			
Combination of above	x	x	x	x
Commodity Futures				x
Options (puts and calls)				x
Banks, Savings and Loans and Credit Unions	x			
Tax Benefit Products				
IRA, Keogh			x	
401(k), ESOP			x	
Annuities			x	
Real Estate	x	x	x	x
Gas and Oil	x	x	x	x
Collectibles		x		x
Gambling, Lotto, etc.				x

CONSIDERATIONS
Phase In Life • Goal Matching • Type Investor • Yield • Safety (Risks) • Liquidity • Taxes • Diversifying

Page 117 may look confusing. So many options and considerations! Where do we start? What are some of the things we need to consider? How can we do a better job without losing our shirt?

Well, you won't become an expert investor overnight after reading this chapter. But, you will be smarter and hopefully a bit wiser. Thus far we have offered you many basic investment insights. Hopefully you realize that these are just the tip of the iceberg .... and there is much more to learn and apply. Read on for a few key things to consider with any investment.

Safety basically means two things: Your chances of making money on your investment, and the chances (or risks) of losing part or all of your money. Do you realize that some investments are more of a gamble than others, that you may very well lose money? Did anyone ever tell you that you should be careful about taking unreasonable gambles with money you can't afford to lose?

Key Investment Questions

Here are just a few questions that wise money managers consider regarding various investments: Is the account federally insured and, if so, to what amount? Are there any guarantees? Are there any "strings" attached? What has been the historical track record of the investment and the organization offering it? What about recently? What prospects does it hold for the future? What has the stock market been doing? Where is it headed? How will this investment be affected by the stock market and the rest of the economy?

These are just a few of the questions to consider when getting a feel for the safety of an investment.

Matching Investments with Goals

Using tax-deferred 401(k) investments for short term goals would cost you much money in taxes and penalties when you take the money out. And, using a federally insured passbook savings account to accumulate all of your retirement assets would generate very conservative earnings but would be very safe, up to the limit insured.

Some investments are more liquid than others. You may need quick access to a certain amount of your assets some day. So, matching these emergency needs and certain other short-term goals to liquid income-type investments would be a wise move.

On the other hand, you may be able to earn better returns with assets in certain tax-deferred or tax exempt investments. These may be better suited to your longer-term goals, especially retirement goals.

Certain growth investments should be appropriate with some of your mid- and/or long-term goals.

What Type of Investor Are You?

The investment objectives and vehicles which are appropriate for you may change as you get older and move through different stages of life and financial status. For example, as your wealth accumulates and you near retirement, you may wish to move more of your assets into safer investments with lower returns. The increase in security may be well worth the decrease in returns.

Are you an aggressive, conservative or very conservative investor? What kind you are depends on your phase in life, how you think about money and several other factors. The type of investor you are can change throughout life as indicated in the retirement example just above.

Do the next exercise to determine the kind of investor you are at this time in your life. Place an x in the boxes that apply to you.

Very Conservative	Conservative	Aggressive
❏ You are older with less time to save for the future.	❏ You are younger, with more time to save for the future.	❏ You are younger or older, with ample funds put aside for the future.
❏ You have 3 or more dependents.	❏ You have 0-2 dependents.	❏ You have 0-1 dependents.
❏ One or both spouses has a low risk tolerance.	❏ You have more time to devote to studying investment opportunities.	❏ You are very familiar with market trends and cycles, and subscribe (or have access) to stock market timing services.
❏ You are seeking to increase your emergency fund or forced savings fund as your primary investment vehicles.	❏ One or both spouses is willing to tolerate some risk in some investments.	❏ You have little resistance to risk, in view of the opportunity to make larger profits.
❏ You are primarily interested in income oriented investments.	❏ You are somewhat knowledgable about the market, enough to take advantage of switching opportunities (investments).	❏ You are willing to trade off safety and liquidity for yield.
❏ Safety is more important than yield (growth) in your investments.	❏ You are interested in growth, tax benefit and speculative objectives as well as income investments.	❏ You will consider speculative as well as other types of investments.
❏ You are willing to trade off some yield for more liquidity.	❏ Safety is secondary to yield.	❏ You can allow your money to be tied up anywhere from 6 months to 5-10 years if necessary.
❏ You are less likely to invest in speculative ventures.	❏ You are willing to let your money be tied up in an investment for at least 6-12 months, if necessary.	❏ You are just as likely to invest in long-term investments as you are in short-term ones.
❏ You are likely to invest in short-term rather than long-term opportunities.	❏ You are just as likely to invest in medium to long-term opportunities as in short-term ones.	❏ You can tolerate maximum losses in stock value (50-100%).
❏ You can tolerate minimal losses in stock value (5-20%).	❏ You can tolerate moderate losses in stock value (15-30%).	

The column you check the most boxes in suggests the type investor that you are at this time.

Final Tips

In addition, the old saying of "don't put all your eggs in one basket" has much wisdom in it. Depending upon the investment(s), to have all of your assets in one or two investments could be taking a real gamble. Wise diversification of your investments helps to "spread" the risks of incurring major losses and damages to your wealth.

So, take the time to learn about and study the many investment options available. Do your homework before you make a new investment, change investments, sell one, or begin "playing" the market.

Refer to the appendix for a list of books, and other money management resources that should be helpful to do a better job of making your money work for you.

Run your life like a business, which includes developing and using a good advisory board. Your board members may change over time. They may include legal, tax, insurance and accounting professionals. Choose and use them wisely.

Don't Touch Your Goal Funds Until Ready, especially retirement funds

We can't warn you enough to resist dipping into your goal funds. Dipping destroys the power of compounding and can set you up for huge taxes and penalties on tax deferred investments.

In this day and age of pension plans being replaced by 401(k) and ESOP plans, employees leaving such companies (whether by choice or not) may leave with fairly large sums of stock and or other assets. If you are not retiring, you should strongly consider "rolling-over" these assets into another tax-deferred investment for retirement. If you don't, the taxes and penalties can cost 40-50% of the total before it even gets to your pocket! Many people are taking the penalties to get at the money and then foolishly spending what's left. After the binge, little or nothing is left for retirement. These people will be poor (and perhaps homeless) in the future in their golden years!

You now know how to keep this from happening to you. But, as you know, knowledge isn't everything!

Step 4: Do It!

Now comes the true challenge--implementing your action plans to achieve your goals.   Read and reread this chapter and the others. Then, start doing things step by step.

Refer To:

❏　Continuously monitor your way of thinking about money. Strive to fine-tune and build better (more solid) foundations for more effective money management.

Chapter 2

❏　Develop some good goals and plans to achieve them.

Chapter 6 and 7

❏　Squeeze your budget and strive to operate on goal-driven budgeting.

Chapters 3, 4 and 5

❏　Save and invest your goal money regularly.

Chapters 5 and 7

❏　Manage your investments according to your goals, phase in life, investment objectives, what you learn over time and other considerations.

Chapter 7

❏　Don't forget about the tax considerations and plan provisions regarding any 401(k) and ESOP assets with payouts.

Chapters 4 and 7

❏　Review and consider the tax consequences on any investment. Consult your accountant or tax attorney to be sure.

❏　Get a good will and living will.

Chapter 4

Remember: In general, not having wills and living wills can rob your survivors of money in the form of taxes, probate and attorney's fees, and/or for needless, often catastrophically expensive medical care that may have no affect on recovery.

❏　Living trusts become more attractive and necessary as the value of your estate becomes bigger.

Chapter 4

❏　Think twice when receiving stock, 401(k) retirement savings, when you win the lotto, receive an inheritance or lose a job.

Chapter 4

Refer To:

❐   Keep on learning. Work to stay aware of your   All Chapters
        money management style, progress, and new   and Appendix
        insights that could help you to better manage
        your money.

❐   Keep track of your readings, programs you   Chart at Right
        attend and advisors (your advisory board)   and Appendix
        regarding the key areas of money management.

        This will help to see areas you are strong in,
        getting stronger in and areas you may need
        some more information on.

❐   Re-read this workbook from time to time.   All Chapters
                                                              and Appendix
❐   Finally, take time out to celebrate the
        achievement of your goals.

        Give yourself and team members recognition
        and appreciation for the hard work and
        discipline invested in making ends meet and
        dreams come true.

Thank you for letting us share these thoughts, tips and
tools with you.

We wish you and your family the best!

Resource Inventory

Place (x) under areas covered by item read, program attended or expertise of advisor.

Sources of Learning and Support	Investing	Insurance	Estate Planning (wills, trusts)	Tax Matters	Goals in $ & Life	Retire-ment	Lifestyle and Thinking	Other Support*

Books/Literature Read

_____ —   —   —   —   —   —   —   —
_____ —   —   —   —   —   —   —   —
_____ —   —   —   —   —   —   —   —
_____ —   —   —   —   —   —   —   —

Programs/Workshops Attended

_____ —   —   —   —   —   —   —   —
_____ —   —   —   —   —   —   —   —
_____ —   —   —   —   —   —   —   —
_____ —   —   —   —   —   —   —   —

Personal Advisors (Contact and Phone)

Accountant

_____ —   —   —   —   —   —   —   —

Insurance Agent(s)

_____ —   —   —   —   —   —   —   —
_____ —   —   —   —   —   —   —   —

Attorney(s)

_____ —   —   —   —   —   —   —   —
_____ —   —   —   —   —   —   —   —

Broker(s)

_____ —   —   —   —   —   —   —   —
_____ —   —   —   —   —   —   —   —

Human Resources-Benefits Contacts

_____ —   —   —   —   —   —   —   —
_____ —   —   —   —   —   —   —   —

Other (wise friends, etc.)

_____ —   —   —   —   —   —   —   —
_____ —   —   —   —   —   —   —   —

Other Resources *   (Contact and Phone)

Local Credit Counseling Agency   _____   nominal fee may be involved
Job Placement Organization   _____
Employee Assistance Service   _____   available through many employers
Local Faith Community   _____   e.g., counseling, food, clothing...
Local American Red Cross, Salv. Army _____ e.g., shelter, food, clothing
County Health Department   _____   e.g., immunizations, health care
Other _____   _____

* Depending upon the resource, a range of support services may be available, such as: counseling (personal, marital and/or family), debt counseling and management, emergency food and/or housing, job placement and medical care.

INDEX

Recommended Resources for Additional Money Management Information and Tools

BOOKS   *For information regarding credit protection laws:*
<u>*CONSUMER HANDBOOK TO CREDIT PROTECTION LAWS:*</u>
Write to the: Board of Governors of the Federal Reserve System, Washington D.C. 10051.

For information about a variety of investments:
<u>*THE EVERYTHING INVESTING BOOK*</u>
by Rich Mintzer and Annette Racond, Adams Media Corporation, 1999

For information about investing in stocks:
<u>*THE WARREN BUFFET WAY*</u>
by Robert G. Hagstrom, Jr., John Wiley and Sons, Inc., 1995

For information about how to invest in mutual funds:
<u>*COMMON SENSE ON MUTUAL FUNDS*</u>
by John C. Bogle, John Wiley and Sons, Inc., 1999

For a great motivational story and inspiration to better manage money:
<u>*THE RICHEST MAN IN BABYLON*</u>
by George S. Clason, Signet Book Penguin Group (New York, NY) 1926.

WEB SITES   *For daily updates and events in the financial world:*
<u>*www.cbsmarketwatch.com*</u>

<u>*www.reuters.com*</u>

For general information and links on a variety of money management topics:
<u>*finance.yahoo.com*</u>

<u>*www.financialinfoportal.com*</u>

SOFTWARE   *Available through many computer software stores and catalogs:*

<u>*MICROSOFT MONEY*</u>

<u>*QUICKEN PERSONAL FINANCE*</u>

MAGAZINES   *For general money management articles at most libraries, bookstores and newstands:*

<u>*MONEY MAGAZINE*</u>

<u>*KIPLINGER's CHANGING TIMES*</u>

<u>*SMART MONEY*</u>

NEWSLETTERS   *You can request a catalog of Money Management Newsletters. The catalog describes the purpose of approximately 100 newsletters. For $69.00 you can get a sample of 4 different newsletters (for 5 months) to see if it is appropriate for you.*

Write to: Select Information Exchange
224 West 54th Street • Suite 614
New York, NY 10019
(212) 247-7123

Available Training and Support Resources
— from the Authors

Core Skills Training in Money Management

Making Ends Meet and Dreams Come True Resources

Standard and Custom Versions — book, video and other resources (below)
Population-Wide Training Initiatives — employees, members, recruits

Worksite Training Seminars and Programs — via onsite trainers, web casts
Video Training Resources — for worksites and homes
Mail-Based Training Initiatives

Train-the-Trainer Workshops
　　　　　Video Training Kits — for Training Leaders
　　　　　Powerpoint Presentation Tools

Advanced/Comprehensive Skills Training

Financial Lifecycle Training Workshops & Resources
Worksite Training Seminars and Programs

Retirement Planning Workshops & Resources
Worksite Training Seminars and Programs

Other Related Training Workshops, Resources & Online Support

Health Risk Management and Loss Control Services
Consumer Health and Patient Safety Training and Tools — for better health care and results
Medical Self-Care Training and Resources — for handling health problems better
Online Decision Support — health, work/family and benefits decision content, tools and sites

For more information contact:

Gary Tagtmeier, CPA, RIA
Financial Awareness® Institute
630-963-7000
www.financialinfoportal.com

Bob Gorsky, PhD
HPN WorldWide, Inc.
630-941-9030
www.hpn.com